The

Choices

We

Made

The

25 Women and Men

Choices

Speak Out About

We

Abortion

Made

Edited and with an introduction by

Angela

Bonavoglia

FOUR WALLS EIGHT WINDOWS
NEW YORK/LONDON

Published in the United States by
Four Walls Eight Windows
39 West 14th Street, room 503
New York, NY 10011
http://www.4W8W.com

UK offices:
Four Walls Eight Windows/Turnaround
Unit 3 Olympia Trading Estate
Coburg Road, Wood Green
London N22 6TZ

The work was originally published in hardcover by Random House, Inc. in 1991 and in paperback in 1992. The first Four Walls Eight Windows paperback edition published in February 2001.

"Kathy" by Angela Bonavoglia was originally published in different form as "Kathy's Day in Court" in the April 1988 issue of *Ms.* magazine.

Grateful acknowledgement is made to the following for permission to reprint previously published material:

Baltimore Evening Sun: Article by Bess Armstrong from the April 26, 1989 issue of the *Baltimore Evening Sun.* Reprinted by permission of the *Baltimore Evening Sun.*

Bourne Company and Music Sales Corporation: Excerpts from "Swinging on a Star" by Johnny Burke and Jimmy Van Heusen. Copyright 1944 (renewed) by Dorsey Brothers Music, a division of Music Sales Corporation, and Bourne Company. International copyright secured. Reprinted by permission of Bourne Company and Music Sales Corporation.

Grove Weidenfeld: "The Princess" from *Dancing at the Edge of the World* by Ursula K. Le Guin. Copyright ©1989 by Ursula K. Le Guin. Reprinted by permission of Grove Weidenfeld.

Rivers Oram Press Limited: Essay by Rayna Rapp from "XYLO: A True Story," from *Test Tube Women: What Future Motherhood?*, edited by Rita Arditti, Renate Klein, and Shelley Minden, Pandora Press, 1984. Reprinted by permission of Rivers Oram Press.

Library of Congress Cataloging-in-Publication Data:

The choices we made: twenty-five women and men speak out about abortion/ edited and with an introduction by Angela Bonavoglia.—1st ed
   p. cm.
     Originally published: New York: Random House, 1991.
     ISBN 1-56858-188-2
     1. Pro-choice movement—United States. 2. Abortion—United States.
I. Title: Twenty-five women and men speak out about abortion. II. Bonavoglia, Angela.

HQ767.5.U5 C48 2001
363.46'0973   —dc21
                                 00-052782

Printed in the United States of America
10 9 8 7 6 5 4 3 2 1

For My Mother

The Court has recognized that a right of personal privacy, or a guarantee of certain areas or zones of privacy, does exist under the Constitution. In varying contexts, the Court or individual Justices have, indeed, found at least the roots of that right in the First Amendment; in the Fourth and Fifth Amendments; in the penumbras of the Bill of Rights; or in the concept of liberty guaranteed by the first section of the Fourteenth Amendment. . . . This right of privacy . . . is broad enough to encompass a woman's decision whether or not to terminate her pregnancy.

> *Justice Blackmun*
> *U.S. Supreme Court*
> *Majority Opinion*
> Roe *v.* Wade
> *January 22, 1973*

I fear for the future. I fear for the liberty and equality of the millions of women who have lived and come of age in the 16 years since *Roe* was decided. . . . For today, at least, the law of abortion stands undisturbed. For today, the women of this Nation still retain the liberty to control their destinies. But the signs are evident and very ominous, and a chill wind blows.

> *Justice Blackmun*
> *U.S. Supreme Court*
> *Dissenting Opinion*
> Webster *v.* Reproductive Health Services
> *July 3, 1989*

Roe continues to exist, but only in the way a storefront on a western movie set exists: a mere facade to give the illusion of reality. . . . We believe that *Roe* was wrongly decided, and that it can and should be overruled.

> *Chief Justice Rehnquist, with*
> *Justices White, Scalia, and Thomas*
> *U.S. Supreme Court*
> *Concurring in Part, Dissenting in Part*
> Planned Parenthood of Southeastern
>   Pennsylvania *v.* Robert P. Casey
> *June 29, 1992*

F o r e w o r d

b y G l o r i a S t e i n e m

You have in your hands a rare example of people telling the simple, complicated, novelistic, stranger-than-fiction truth about their lives.

Stories like these seldom get published. The emotional toll of telling is too great, or the stories themselves are considered too intimate, too personal. Yet they are part of a long tradition. From the prisoners whose stories started the storming of the Bastille and the French revolution to the "speaking bitterness" groups of China, from the church "testifying" that started the civil rights movement to the consciousness-raising that began this most recent wave of feminism, populist truth-telling has been the heart and soul of movements and revolutions all over the world. ———————

For one thing, it's the basic building block of change. Revolutions, like houses, can only be built from the bottom up. For another, it's contagious. I doubt that many readers will get through this book without feeling the urge to share the similar stories that have touched their lives.

I for one cannot. My own abortion was pivotal in my life; the worst and the best of it; a symbol of fear, but also the first time I stopped passively accepting whatever happened to me and took responsibility. Even disclosing it years later was a turning point.

I had been a good liberal in the 1960s, identifying with every group that was having a hard time, yet never realizing why. As a white and, by then, middle-class person, I assumed that my feelings were just quixotic. Certainly, being a female could not be serious enough to explain them. If I felt endangered while walking in the city streets, that was inevitable—and probably my own fault for being there. If I had trouble renting an apartment or couldn't get a credit card, that was logical, too—women just weren't financial grown-ups. If I didn't get equal pay or political assignments as a journalist, I would have to work harder—and pretend to be more like my male colleagues. When editors did pay me the ultimate compliment of saying, "You write like a man," I felt flattered—and said, "Thank you."

Then in 1969, I went as a reporter to cover an unofficial abortion hearing in New York City. It was an early feminist speak-out, a protest against official hearings on the proposed liberalization of state abortion laws. Fourteen men and one nun had been invited to testify before the legislature. Therefore, the organizers of this speak-out had invited diverse and ordinary women to testify in a church basement before an audience of friends and reporters.

I went to listen, as a journalist—or so I thought. There were stories of sexual abuse; for instance, a woman who had been forced to have sex with the abortionist before he would operate. There were stories of race and class hatred; for instance, a woman who had been bargained with—she could have a legal abortion, but only if she also agreed to be sterilized. There was humiliation at the hands of those in power; for instance, men on a hospital board who made a young woman describe in detail how she got pregnant—and then denied her a legal abortion anyway. There was a tragic amount of misinformation and even humor. One woman had believed her boyfriend who insisted that she couldn't get pregnant from a second ejaculation, and others confessed to having believed similar myths. But there were also accounts of extraordinary courage and extraordinary hypocrisy. For instance, a legendary Pennsylvania doctor testified that policemen and politicians sent him their wives and daughters for abortions, even though he had been arrested several times.

In all these stories, there was honesty—and it amazed me. For the first time, I was hearing women tell the truth in public. And for the first time, I was hearing female experience taken seriously.

Suddenly, I began to wonder: If one in three or four American women had an abortion at some time in her life—a common statistical estimate, even in those days of its illegality—then why, *why* should this single surgical procedure be deemed a criminal act?

Like a ball of yarn that unravels from one strand to its very heart, this question led to the core of patriarchy and the reasons why the freedom of women as a group was restricted. It was men's need to own children that had made some "legitimate" and some "illegitimate"; it was the need of patriarchal states to control the number of workers and soldiers that had made birth control a privilege instead of a right; it was their need to maintain racial caste systems that drove them to restrict when and with whom women could have children; in short, it was women's bodies as the most basic means of production, the means of reproduction, that had always been the object of this deep political game. No wonder we met such opposition when we asked simply to decide our own sexual and physical futures. We were seizing control of the means of reproduction. It sounded radical—and it was.

Indeed, I don't think we realized how radical until the full force of religious and secular patriarchy began to organize against reproductive freedom, using everything from churches as political centers to terrorist bombers of abortion clinics.

After that speak-out, I wrote what on looking back seems a rather mild article called "After Black Power, Women's Liberation." I was still writing in the third person, concealing my experience as my male colleagues did (although they disapproved of this article nonetheless—several took me aside to warn me that writing favorably about these "crazy women" would endanger my hard-won status as a "seriousness" reporter). So what this article didn't explain was that I, too, had had an abortion, shortly after I got out of college. I had gone through it totally alone, out of both humiliation and pride. I had not told the man, whose feelings I didn't want to hurt, or my mother, whose fragile state of mind I needed to protect. No parental/paternal notification or consent law would have made me tell them. I was twenty-two, but I still would have endangered my life for privacy. It was a first and long overdue effort to control my own destiny.

In fact, sixteen years later, when I finally told my mother about that abortion, the motive was not coercion but hope. The first issue of *Ms.* magazine was going to include a list of many notable American women who admitted that they had had abortions and asked for a repeal of all anti-abortion laws. I couldn't ask others to be truthful if I was not, so before I signed, I had to tell my family. We became closer—thanks to feminism, not to force.

Like each story in these pages, mine is unique. I think you will be amazed by the diversity of experience, motive, and thought represented here. Yet in mine and every story there are common threads that extend to readers far beyond the boundaries of this country.

In the anti-Communist revolution of Eastern Europe, for instance, reproductive freedom was as basic a demand as freedom of speech or assembly. In response to the forced birth policies and inhuman baby wards of Romania, men and women marched with banners that read "Democracy and Abortion," the motto of their revolution. In the Soviet Union, where economic problems and racist concerns have made abortion almost the *only* form of family planning, freely available contraception is now a symbol of new democracy.

Reproductive freedom—the right to decide when and whether to have children—is also the central goal of Irish and Iranian women who smuggle contraceptives into their theocratic countries and smuggle out their sisters who need abortions or tubal ligations. It is the goal of women and men in China who rebel against the government dictating that all couples have only one child. It is the hope of African and Middle Eastern women who work not only for contraception and safe birthing conditions, but against genital mutilation. It is the political issue that is galvanizing governments and elections, from the United States and Brazil to Italy and Japan.

Make no mistake, these are not "little" stories. They are voices in a worldwide chorus that is adding the female half of humanity to the goal of global democracy.

And the point of democracy is not: *What* gets decided? The point is: *Who* decides?

A c k n o w l e d g m e n t s

The efforts and support of many people made this book possible. With that in mind, I extend my deepest appreciation to:

Gloria Steinem for envisioning the idea and believing I could turn it into a reality, and Mary Thom for sharing that belief.

All of the people who spoke to me about their experiences for their incredible honesty, commitment, and courage.

The men and women all over the country who helped with this project, especially in finding the voices for the book, including Steven Barclay, Janet Benshoof, Marilyn Bergman, Donna Brazile, Anita DeFrance, Joan Dunlop, Susan Dworkin, Kit Everett, Maureen Fenlon, Sara Friedman, Sydney Goldstein, Doug Gould, Aileen Hernandez, Jane Hodgson, M.D., Frances Kidd, Kristina Kiehl, Jon Knowles, Deborah Landau, Suzanne Levine, Marla Ludwig, Luz Alvarez Martinez, Jane Ordway, U.S. Senator Bob Packwood, Barbara Radford, Tamar Rafael, Sue Roselle, Loretta Ross, Polly Rothstein, Roberta Synal, Marge Tabankin, Susan Tew, California State Senator Diane E. Watson, and Gretchen Wright.

My editor, Becky Saletan, for her patience, enthusiasm, and encouragement, and former *Ms.* editors Joanne Edgar and Gloria Jacobs for their encouragement years ago, which enabled me to grow.

Friends and colleagues from the Ms. Foundation for Women, especially Sara Gould, Marie Wilson, Susan Dickler, Pat Bronstein, Cindy Gibson, and Carol Yesalonis (who so patiently transcribed all these many hours of tape), and from Beth Israel Medical Center, especially Jane G. Blumenfeld, Stephen Burke, and Dave Perrett.

Other friends who are my family: Claude Barilleaux, Rose Brown, Jean Brewer, Rochelle Green, Phil Garrison, Nancy Wartik, Donna Dunlop, Patricia Read, Amy Pouser Webb, Skip Webb, Judy Lopatin, Andrea Pedolsky, Marilyn Scott, Jason Scott, Sandi and Jerry Klein, the Mirandas, and everyone at St. Ann's.

And finally, Robbie and Jim Bonavoglia, and my mother, Frances B. Bianco, for absolutely everything.

Contents

Introduction

The U.S. Supreme Court's 1973 landmark decision, *Roe v. Wade*, made abortion safe and legal. Gone were the days of skulking and sneaking, hiding and lying, traveling to unknown addresses in unmarked cars, having "surgery" without an anesthetic, and surrendering to the hands of charlatans and opportunists. Gone was the risk to thousands of women's lives each year.

But the victory was short-lived. By the mid-1970s, an increasingly well organized grassroots anti-choice movement had emerged. While the tactics of its most powerful organizations were mainstream, directed primarily at influencing politics and laws, by the early 1980s, far more militant anti-choice groups had formed. As a result of their efforts, many women who exercised their constitutional right to make one of the most difficult decisions of their lives and sought abortions were shut out at the door. So-called pro-life forces blockaded clinic entrances, taunted and harassed women and their families, kidnapped clinic workers, issued death threats, and set fire to or bombed clinic after clinic, in city after city.

Not only did the U.S. government refuse to protect a woman's right; it actively joined the opposition. In 1989, the federal government argued before the Supreme Court in *Webster v. Reproductive Health Services* to abolish a woman's right to choose by overturning *Roe*. While the Court in *Webster* stopped short of doing that, it shocked America by giving states the right to uphold pernicious restrictions on choice and, most important, attacking *Roe*'s Solomonesque attempt to balance the interests of the mother, the fetus, and the state.

Roe had never given women an unfettered right to abortion throughout pregnancy. It authorized state regulation—after the first three months of pregnancy to protect the woman's health, and after fetal viability (about twenty-four weeks) to protect the fetus, provided that did not endanger the woman's life or health. But a plurality of the Court in *Webster* said that it saw "no reason why the State's compelling interest in protecting potential human life should not extend throughout pregnancy."

Many state legislatures read the decision as an engraved invitation to renew efforts to outlaw abortion. By early 1992, at least four hundred bills regulating abortion had been introduced, including mandatory delays, state-scripted lectures, and outright bans. *Planned Parenthood of Southeastern Pennsylvania v. Robert P. Casey* was the first of the post-*Webster* cases promoting state restrictions to reach the U.S. Supreme Court.

Surprising the pundits, a new majority of five justices formed in the *Casey* decision to defend *Roe*, concluding that "the essential holding of *Roe v. Wade* should be retained and once again reaffirmed." The victory, however, was more imagined than real. The court in *Casey* upheld most of Pennsylvania's meddlesome abortion restrictions. It also rejected the trimester framework and, for the first time since *Roe*, authorized states to institute abortion regulations throughout pregnancy in order to discourage the procedure. Only restrictions determined to pose an "undue burden" would be held unconstitutional. Finally, the margin of victory—one justice's vote—was perilously slim. In *Casey*, four justices went on record saying that *Roe* had been "wrongly decided, and that it can and should be overruled."

In the face of these unprecedented threats to legal abortion, pro-choice forces came out of a slumber and mobilized. In the year *Webster* was decided, they marched 300,000 strong into Washington, D.C. Three years later, just before *Casey*, they doubled their numbers, holding one of the largest demonstrations that the nation's capital had ever seen.

Deeply concerned about these threats to choice and their implications for women's lives, the women and men in this book came forward to bear witness. Admitting to personal experience regarding a matter as controversial as abortion takes enormous courage. That is what fifty-three notable American women did in 1972 when they signed their names to a legislative petition published in *Ms.* magazine inviting other women to join them, and what nearly 350 French women did the year before when they signed and published a similar statement. It also takes courage to tell one's story anonymously. Those who lend their names and tell their stories—as have nearly all those included here—are possessed of double courage. By making that choice, they have helped to create a singular personal and historical record of the struggle for reproductive rights.

• • •

In the decade since *The Choices We Made* was first published, the battle over abortion has turned deadly. Dr. David Gunn was murdered as he entered his Pensacola, Florida, clinic in 1993, making him the first abortion-provider fatality. Anti-abortion extremist Paul Hill shot and killed Dr. John Bayard Britton and his clinic escort, James Barrett, the next year, in the same city. Also in 1994, John Salvi gunned down Planned Parenthood receptionist Shannon Lowney in Brookline, Massachusetts, shot and killed another receptionist, Leanne Nichols, and then wounded five more people. A bomb packed with nails exploded at a women's health clinic in Birmingham, Alabama, at the beginning of 1998, killing security guard Robert Sanderson and maiming a nurse, and the year ended with the sniper shooting death of Dr. Barnett Slepian in his own home in Amherst, New York. Major suspects in this violence remain at large.

But the nineties also saw a transfer of the reins of American government to a pro-choice president, which armed pro-choice forces with new and potent weapons in the battle for reproductive rights. In 1994, former president William Jefferson Clinton signed into law the Freedom of Access to Clinic Entrances Act, which made it a crime for anyone "by force, threat of force or physical obstruction" to intentionally injure, intimidate, or interfere with someone obtaining or providing reproductive health services. The Supreme Court, state legislatures, and municipalities approved the establishment of "buffer" zones of safety for women and staff outside of clinics, which circumscribe the distance between demonstrators and their targets. The Supreme Court also affirmed the use of federal racketeering laws to bring charges against the leaders of anti-abortion organizations for engaging in patterns of fear, intimidation, and unlawful activities to drive clinics out of business.

These developments led to the successful prosecution of

many perpetrators of clinic violence, a stepped-up response by law enforcement agencies, and a dramatic decline in clinic blockades. In addition, the U.S. Food and Drug Administration approved emergency contraception (hormonal medications that prevent pregnancy if taken within seventy-two hours of unprotected intercourse) and the drug RU-486 (an early alternative to surgical abortion), actions sure to reshape the landscape in years to come. Still, in 1999, vandalism raged, and one out of every five clinics reported incidents of death threats, stalkings, bombings, break-ins, chemical attacks, and arson. For the short run, at least, the damage had been done: 86 percent of the counties in the United States had not a single abortion provider.

Along with the violence came vilification. Increasingly frustrated anti-choice activists began to openly defend murder and maiming as tactics in their self-anointed holy war. They went so far as to distribute "wanted" posters featuring photos, names, and addresses of physicians who performed abortions. They mounted a "Nuremberg Files" Internet website with the same information, drawing lines through the names of murdered physicians and shading the names of the wounded in grey.

Anti-choice leaders also began to vilify as never before women who have abortions. Rather than focus on women who end pregnancies early on (nearly 90 percent of the 1.3 million procedures done annually take place in the first twelve weeks), they demonized the most vulnerable women, those who have later procedures. In fact, young, poor women whose access to abortion is impeded by state restrictions are often the ones who have second-trimester abortions. As for the latest procedures, they are allowable only for severe fetal abnormality or to protect the mother's health or life.

Women who aborted late in pregnancy for severe fetal anomaly bravely testified against a federal ban on so-called partial birth abortions before the House Judiciary Committee in

1995. They were accused by committee members of being part of "a radical fringe"; one woman was called "an exterminator." Palpably expressing its disdain, the National Council of Catholic Bishops supported the legislation with a full-page ad in the *Washington Post* denouncing the woman who has a later abortion of doing so because she "hates being fat," "can't afford a baby and a new car," or "won't fit into prom dress." Within two years, thirty-one states had passed partial birth abortion bans, a frenzy halted only when the U.S. Supreme Court, in *Stenberg v. Carhart*, declared the Nebraska ban—written so broadly that it would have outlawed any abortion procedure—to be unconstitutional.

Against this backdrop of violence and vilification come the voices in this book. In their quiet and powerful narratives, they remind us of the women who stand alone at the center of this storm, each struggling in her own moral context to make the right decision, women who are not, as the anti-choice zealots would have us believe, alien and apart. In fact, they are, as they have always been, our mothers, our grandmothers, and our great-grandmothers. More than half of the women who have abortions have already given birth. Two-thirds of the women who have had an abortion plan to have a child or more children in the future. At the time I interviewed the women in this book, they had, collectively, mothered fifty-two biological, adopted, and step-sons and step-daughters, and had twenty-eight grandchildren and six great-grandchildren.

Actress Anne Archer said she participated in this project because "It is only through the personal stories of women who have had abortions that we will come to understand what the human experience is," and indeed, this book is about that human experience. It is about making the abortion decision, the procedure itself, the aftermath, and the meaning of abortion in people's lives. It is about the force of a woman's determination to end a pregnancy when she feels she must, and the suffering that can follow when the procedure she seeks is made illegal and unsafe.

In fact, many of the stories in this book—told primarily in each person's own words, as oral history—provide valuable documentation of the circumstances under which women had illegal abortions through seven decades, from the 1920s through the 1980s. The stories fill in the historical canvas with the details of specific experiences, in the context of changing mores and social conditions.

Retired Marine master sergeant Jim Friedl recalls witnessing his twenty-seven-year-old mother's death at home from an overdose of a drug she had taken to abort. At that time—the 1920s—abortion had only relatively recently become illegal throughout the United States. In fact, abortions prior to the point of "quickening"—that is, when the pregnant woman first feels fetal movement, generally around eighteen to twenty weeks—were permitted by traditional common law until the middle of the 1800s. But by 1900, every state in the country had outlawed abortion, a movement fueled by "nativism"— anti-immigrant fear that too few white Protestant children were being born—as well as stepped-up pressure by the medical profession to drive charlatans and competitors out of business and gain greater control over medical care.

In 1930, the year after Friedl's mother died, abortion was the official cause of death for nearly 2,700 American women, representing 18 percent of all maternal deaths, though it is generally agreed that unreported deaths from illegal abortion make the actual number much higher. In 1965, illegal abortion still accounted for almost 17 percent of all deaths related to pregnancy and childbirth, and 55 percent of those who died were women of color. Today, deaths from legal abortion in the United States are extremely rare (less than one per 100,000). However, of the more than 500,000 women who die annually from maternity-related causes worldwide—nearly all in the developing world—an estimated 15 percent or 78,000 die from unsafe abortions.

Some women in this book had illegal abortions at the hands of kind and caring physicians who put their professional lives on the line. But many had abortions that were terrifying back alley affairs. The woman who came to actress Margot Kidder's hotel room administered what turned out to be Lysol. Pat Tyson, former director of the Religious Coalition for Abortion Rights, bled so severely that she needed transfusions. And actress Polly Bergen had a procedure that ultimately cost her fertility.

Women talked about taking black pills, and clear pills that looked like vitamin E, and mixtures of toxic ingredients they'd been told about—like the concoction of Clorox, baking soda, cream, and Johnny Walker Red that Whoopi Goldberg took when she was only fourteen. They talked about abortionists using various implements to dilate the cervix, leaving the implements inside and "packing" the women with gauze, and of having D&Cs (dilation and curettage), without an anesthetic.

Legalization eliminated much of the danger of abortion, but it also raised a whole spectrum of new and difficult issues. The stories in the second section of this book focus on those issues, which include unequal access to legal abortion, the dilemmas posed by the new medical technologies, and the unacknowledged emotional and spiritual needs of women who have abortions.

"Kathy" was the teen who in 1987 challenged Alabama's parental consent law, which required minors who could not go to their parents for consent for an abortion to request the permission of a judge. At that time, some 5,000 young women had appeared in Massachusetts Superior Adult Court requesting permission to have an abortion from the same judges who heard cases of fraud, blackmail, armed robbery, felony assault, rape, and murder, and another 3,500 had gone through the Minnesota courts. By the year 2000, nearly three-quarters of the states had on the books some form of parental consent or notification statute. The first known casualty of the laws was seventeen-year-old Rebecca Bell of Indiana, who, afraid to tell her parents or go to court, died from infection and pneumonia caused by a botched illegal abortion.

Another story in this section concerns a young woman, daughter of a well-known journalist, who was brutally gang-raped and impregnated. Her father tells the story of her terrible ordeal, including his ire over a senate committee's proposal to extend the ban on Medicare coverage for poor women's abortions to cases of rape and incest. He was also outraged that the hospital to which he took his daughter after the attack refused to give her the "morning after pill," a concentrated dose of ordinary birth control pills that would have prevented her pregnancy. Though the FDA has since approved the morning after pill, now called emergency contraception, virulent opposition to the intervention continues. Some pharmacists refuse to fill prescriptions, and many emergency rooms in the United States will not dispense the medication to rape victims.

Other medical advances have raised new dilemmas for pregnant women and their partners. Amniocentesis, for example, can only be done after sixteen weeks of pregnancy; if a severe disability is found in the fetus, the mother who chooses not to carry the pregnancy to term has no recourse but a late abortion. Anthropologist Rayna Rapp tells of the heartache she suffered when faced with that choice, and actress Bess Armstrong shares her feelings about the same difficult issue.

Amid the fierce controversy over abortion today, it is easy to lose sight of the highly personal nature of the decision to end a pregnancy—the basic right upheld by *Roe*—and the enormous emotional impact that decision can have on the woman who makes it. This emotional denial represents one of the most universal hardships imposed on women who have abortions, which actress and writer Kathy Najimy describes as a woman's right "to feel bad without feeling wrong."

The spiritual dimension of the abortion experience has also been denied, with religious ground being ceded by many on the pro-choice side to intolerant Catholic theologians and Christian fundamentalists. That is ironic, for—as activist Judy Widdicombe in her story attests—clergy from a wide range of denominations saved many women's lives when abortion was illegal by courageously establishing the Clergy Consultation Service, offering counseling and referral programs nationwide.

Many of those I interviewed talked about their concepts of God and spirituality, and the relationship of those concepts to choice. The Reverend Christine Grimbol, a Presbyterian minister, offered a view of the message of Christ that contrasts dramatically with the anti-choice preaching of the fundamentalists. Her account of her struggle for a spiritual context for her legal abortion raises issues that affect women of all denominations and creeds.

Those in the book who had grown up Catholic typically suffered great conflict about abortion. They spoke for the many Catholic women who, in spite of the Catholic church's absolute prohibition, are as likely as all women nationally to have an abortion, and in fact, are 29 percent more likely to do so than Protestant women. It is interesting to note that the Catholic prohibition was not always so absolute. From AD 1150 to the nineteenth century, Catholic canon law held that abortion of an "unformed" embryo—up to forty days for a male and eighty for a female (it was thought that the male fetus quickened earlier)—was not murder, though it was considered a sexual sin. For centuries, Catholic theologians taught that ensoulment did not occur until the embryo began to show human form.

In addition to documenting individual experiences, the stories in this book also reveal the diverse feelings and beliefs of those who take a pro-choice stand. You will hear agreement on the basic principle of a woman's right to choose to end a pregnancy, as well as an abiding belief in her moral ability to decide. But you will also hear a passionate and disparate range of opinion that dispels any notion that there is a single pro-choice voice.

The women I spoke with told me candidly of their emotional reactions to the abortion experience, which ranged from terror and confusion to resignation, peace, and most often, relief. No woman in the book described herself as suffering lifelong psychological damage as a result of her abortion. This is in keeping with the findings of scientific studies on the psychological responses to legal abortion in the United States, which show that "severe negative reactions" are infrequent. Even the report commissioned by former president Ronald Reagan and carried out by then-surgeon general C. Everett Koop could find no conclusive evidence of adverse psychological reactions to abortion.

Likewise, I heard a range of beliefs about when life begins. Some women felt that life as we understand it is not present during the embryonic stage, in the first few weeks of pregnancy. For journalist Linda Ellerbee, "life in a certain sense probably does begin at conception, even perhaps right before conception—the properties of life are in the sperm and they're in the womb." Others were more definite on the point. "A fetus is alive from the moment of conception," said actress Jill Clayburgh. "I don't think that we should say it isn't alive until such and such a week or month. . . . The position is not about whether or not it's alive; it's about whether or not someone wants to give birth and have the responsibility of another human being with them for the rest of their life."

While all agreed with Roe's authorization of state restrictions on abortion after fetal viability, some of those I talked to articulated their own dividing lines. Several were disturbed by the prospect of second-trimester abortions, yet they felt they could not impose their beliefs on others, particularly on women who had been raped, who were victims of incest, or who faced the anguishing decision of whether or not to carry a fetus with disabilities to term.

The vast majority of the women in this book had abortions when they were young and unmarried, characteristics still shared by the majority of women who have abortions. In that regard, the stories in this book provide ample evidence that a society's attitudes toward abortion cannot be separated from that society's attitudes toward sexuality, particularly female sexuality. Many of the women attested to beginning their sexual lives poorly prepared and ill educated. Sex was simply not discussed at home or at school, partly because of general discomfort with the subject, and partly because it wasn't acknowledged that "good girls" needed any such instruction.

"More than anything else, what scared me about getting pregnant was the shame of being found out as being a 'bad girl,'" says actress Rita Moreno, who had an abortion in the 1950s. "The shame of being pregnant out of wedlock was so profound, . . . it was a kind of terrorism that was practiced upon young women." Indeed, the issue of shame rises over and over again in these pages—shame over being sexual, shame over being pregnant outside of marriage, shame over having had a back alley abortion, shame over having had any abortion at all.

In addition to—and largely because of—mores that forbade young women to be sexual, the women in this book inherited an arcane knowledge of human sexuality and birth control. Some of the women learned about pregnancy prevention from men, who learned from other men and were fairly ignorant. Archer listened to her boyfriend, who said that foam alone would do the trick (it didn't), and Ellerbee to hers, who said they were in a "safe" time of the month (they weren't). Some women picked up misinformation on their own—writer Nora Sayre and her contemporaries at Radcliffe depended on foam—and some invented their own remedies.

It must be remembered, of course, that for much of the period during which abortion was illegal, birth control was illegal or very hard for an unmarried woman to get. Anthony Comstock—champion of censorship and organizer of the New York Society for the Suppression of Vice—campaigned in the late 1800s against contraceptives. He succeeded in getting the federal government to define birth control drugs and devices as obscene and to ban both their sale and the dissemination of information about them through the mail. That prompted many states to pass criminal statutes of their own. It was not until 1965 that the U.S. Supreme Court, in *Griswold v. Connecticut*, struck down all state laws forbidding the use of contraceptives by married couples, based on the right to privacy, and then not until 1972, in *Eisenstadt v. Baird*, was that same right extended to unmarried persons.

Soon, strategies similar to those used to deprive women of birth control information were being used with abortion. In 1988, the Reagan administration proposed a new regulation for workers in federally funded family planning clinics that would forbid them from discussing abortion with their patients. Challenges from pro-choice groups sent the regulation in *Rust v. Sullivan* to the U.S. Supreme Court, which made an astonishing exception to the First Amendment and upheld the so-called gag rule. While the Clinton administration lifted that ban in the United States, agencies abroad in receipt of family planning funds have been gagged and even prohibited from using other funding for abortion counseling.

In spite of their ignorance and the lingering taint of immorality that surrounded the use of birth control, some women in the book did use it. Their pregnancies resulted from misinformation or failure of a method, which included diaphragms, foam, IUDs, the sponge, and the birth control pill. But many did not use contraception. They had never been to a gynecologist and saw such a visit for the express purpose of getting birth control as too intimidating and embarrassing a prospect. Polly Bergen felt that way in 1947, and "Kathy"—among the almost one million teenagers who get pregnant annually in the United

States—felt that way in 1987. Such self-consciousness persists, as does a lack of information about pregnancy prevention (facilitated by the federal government's vigorous support for "abstinence only" sex education) and by laws that intentionally limit a minor's access to confidential, affordable care.

Most of the women kept their pregnancies and abortions a secret from their parents. Some feared physical retaliation, but most wanted to spare their parents stress, worry, or shame. These women kept the silence so that their parents' dreams would not be dashed, dreams of daughters pure and innocent, asexual—and therefore not fully human. It was an impossible dream for most young women to live up to. It still is.

Without the right to be sexual, and with birth control illegal, unavailable, undependable, or "immoral," women have approached their sexual lives like a game of Russian roulette. For those who got "caught," illegal abortion stood as the cruelest punishment of all. Continued efforts to outlaw abortion, especially in the absence of a commitment to better access to birth control and sex education, seek to restore that punishment and thereby tighten the reins on female sexuality once again. But as these stories also attest, neither people nor contraception are perfect, and the recourse of safe and legal abortion must remain.

• • •

This edition of *The Choices We Made* is reprinted exactly as the book appeared when it was published ten years ago. The opening biographies reflect the circumstances of each person's life when he or she chose to participate in the project. Much, of course, has happened in the intervening years. Kay Boyle died at the age of ninety; breast cancer took Danitra Vance at just thirty-five; the Reverend Christine Grimbol died at only fifty-four from surgical complications. The wave of anti-choice sentiment swept up Norma McCorvey, the real "Jane Roe," plaintiff in *Roe v. Wade*, who became a born-again Christian and staunch opponent of choice. Her story in this collection recalls her experience when she was a unique symbol of the pro-choice movement.

Rita Moreno became a grandmother, and Kathy Najimy became a mother. Margot Kidder fell on hard times, emerging as an advocate for alternative treatment for the disease with which she struggles, bipolar disorder. Nora Sayre finished the book she was working on—*Previous Convictions: A Journey through the 1950s*—as did anthropologist Rayna Rapp—*Testing Women, Testing the Fetus: The Social Impact of Amniocentesis in America.* Polly Bergen resumed her singing career, to great reviews; Linda Ellerbee won more television awards; and Anne Archer made more acclaimed films. Whoopi Goldberg became the first woman ever to host the Academy Awards, and Grace Paley did "live long enough," as she had hoped, to write more books. Several of the actresses lit up the small screen—Najimy in *Veronica's Closet*, Moreno in *Oz*, Armstrong in *My So-Called Life*, and Clayburgh in *Ally McBeal.*

Before this book, which began as a glimmer in Gloria Steinem's eye, became a powerful statement of pro-choice voices, we embarked on an exhaustive search for the people who would participate. Some responded quickly with a yes. Some had to give the decision a great deal of thought. Some said no because they feared that it would hurt their mothers, or that sharing their reasoning about having an abortion would threaten the very principle of choice—that the decision to have or not have a child must be a private one. A woman who deeply regretted the abortion she had at her lover's insistence—yielding her choice to his—ultimately decided she could not share that story. By and large, women were more afraid to reveal that they had had a legal than an illegal abortion. "There's a real sympathy for women who had illegal abortions. They're the martyrs," said one. "I feel like a criminal."

With the exception of a few whose writings appear, I met each person in the book face-to-face. *The Choices We Made* became an odyssey for me through the diverse layers of our society and through time, in the company of extraordinary women and men. They ranged in age from eighteen to nearly ninety. We visited in all kinds of settings in different parts of the country—in mansions, apartments, a trailer home, offices, hotels, restaurants, a retirement village, and a church. I sat with Linda Ellerbee on the third floor of her Greenwich Village brownstone while an MTV crew set up downstairs for a documentary Linda would narrate. I talked with Anne Archer in a Manhattan hotel over the grinding sounds of renovation; with the Reverend Christine Grimbol at her Sag Harbor Presbyterian Church on Long Island during a tornado watch; and with writer Kay Boyle in her room at the Redwoods, a retirement community in northern California, when she was so frail she had to lie down to speak. I waited for Barbara Corday in the CBS executive offices in Los Angeles with a room full of handsome young businessmen, thinking how different my business surely was from theirs.

The interviews sometimes began warmly, sometimes guardedly, but all progressed to a common place—the heart of each person's story. Some had never spoken publicly before about their experiences with abortion, and unexpected feelings welled up in them, provoking tears or anger or silence.

I tucked away my tape recorder after each interview, feeling the weight of my precious cargo—and sometimes feeling sad. I remember the loud and lonely echo of my footsteps as I walked down the hall from one interview, which sounded to me like the echo of all the stories I had heard, and all the stories they represented, reverberating throughout history.

I think that, as you read, you will hear the echo, too.

Angela Bonavoglia
New York, January 2001

The

Illegal

Days

Grace Paley

Witty, wry, and beloved storyteller Grace Paley (author of several short story collections—*Enormous Changes at the Last Minute, The Little Disturbances of Man, Later That Same Day*—and more, "if I live long enough") was born to Eastern European Jewish parents in New York City in 1922. Today, she resides with her second husband, Robert Nichols, in Vermont and in Manhattan's Greenwich Village, a neighborhood she has lived in for some forty years.

Paley has two children, three stepchildren, and a granddaughter. In addition to writing, she has been an activist all her life in the movements for peace and women's rights.

It was the late thirties, and we all knew that birth control existed, but we also knew it was impossible to get. You had to be older and married. You couldn't get anything in drugstores, unless you were terribly sick and had to buy it because your womb was falling out. The general embarassment and misery around getting birth control were real.

There was Margaret Sanger at that time, and she had a clinic right here in Manhattan in a beautiful house on Sixteenth Street; I still walk past and look at it. As brave as the Margaret Sanger people were, they were under very tough strictures. It was very

scary to go there. I was eighteen, and it was 1940 when I tiptoed
in to get a diaphragm. I think I went before I was married and
said I was married.

When I was young, it really angered me that birth control was
so hard to get. Kids who were not as sophisticated as us Bronx
kids just didn't know what to do. But I never felt like this was
happening just to me. I had a very good social sense then from
my own political family. I also had a lot of good girlfriends, and
we used to talk about it together. We had in common this
considerable disgust and anger at the whole situation.

I grew up in the Bronx to a puritanical, Socialist, Jewish
family. My mother was very puritanical, and all that sex stuff
was very hard for her to talk about—so she didn't. My father
was a doctor, but we still didn't talk about such things. I really
never felt terribly injured by all that. It just seemed to be the
way it was with all of my friends. We considered ourselves free
thinkers . . . in advance of our parents.

Most of my friends married early. I married when I was
nineteen, then my husband went overseas during the Second
World War. I would have loved it if I had had a child when he
went overseas, but we had decided against it.

When he came back, I was in my late twenties, and in the next
couple of years, I had two children. When the children were one
and a half and three, I got pregnant again. I don't remember if
my birth control failed . . . I wasn't the most careful person in
the world. Something in me did want to have more children, but
since I had never gotten pregnant until I really wanted to get
pregnant—I was twenty-six and a half when I had my first
child—I had assumed that that general mode would continue.

I knew I couldn't have another child. I was exhausted with
these two tiny, little kids; it was just about all I could do to take
care of them. As a child, I had been sick a lot, and people were
always thinking I was anemic . . . I was having bouts of that
kind. I just was very tired, all the time. I knew something was

wrong because my whole idea in my heart had always been to have five, six children—I *loved* the idea of having children—but I knew I couldn't have this kid.

Seeing the state I was in, even my father said, "You must not have another child." That gives you an idea of my parents' view. They didn't feel you had to just keep having babies if you had a lot to do, small children, and not a lot of money.

And my husband and I were having hard times. It was really rough. My husband was not that crazy about having children anyway; it was very low on his list of priorities. We lived where the school is now, right next door here, and were supers of the rooming house. He was just beginning his career. He eventually made documentary films, but he'd come back from the army and was getting it all together, like a lot of those guys. So anyway, it was financially hard. But it was mostly the psychological aspect of it that would have been hard for him.

In the 1930s, my late teens, I really didn't know a lot of people who had had abortions, but then later on—not much later, when I was a young married woman in the 1940s—I heard much more. People would talk about it. By then, women were going all over the place, to this famous guy in Pennsylvania, to Puerto Rico. And you were always hearing about somebody who once did abortions but wasn't there doing them anymore.

I didn't ask my father for help. I wasn't really a kid, stuck and pregnant and afraid that the world would fall down on me. I was a woman with two small children, trying to be independent. I didn't want to distress him. He already wasn't feeling very well; he had a very bad heart. And he really couldn't travel; he lived in the northern Bronx, and I was living on Eleventh Street—it would have been a terrible subway trip. I just didn't want to bother him.

I talked the situation over with the women in the park where I used to hang out with the kids. None of them thought having an abortion was a terrible thing to do. You would say, "I can't have a kid now . . . I can't do it," and everybody was perfectly sympathetic. They said to me, "Ask so and so. She had one recently." I did, and I got a name. The woman didn't say anything about the guy; she just said, "Call." I assumed he was a real doctor, and he was. That may have been luck.

My abortion was a very clean and decent affair, but I didn't know until I got there that it would be all right. The doctor's office was in Manhattan, on West End Avenue. I went during the day, and I went with my husband. The doctor had two or three rooms. My husband sat and waited in one of them. There were other people waiting for other kinds of care, which is how this doctor did it; he did a whole bunch of things. He saw someone ahead of me, and when he put me in another room to rest for a few minutes afterwards, I heard him talking to other patients.

The nurse was there during the procedure. He didn't give me an anesthetic; he said, "If you want it, I'll give it to you, but it will be much safer and better if I don't." It hurt, but it wasn't that painful. So I don't have anything traumatic to say about it. I was angry that I had to become a surreptitious person and that I was in danger, but the guy was very clean, and he was very good, and he was arrested within the next year. He went to jail.

I didn't feel bad about the abortion. I didn't have the feelings that people are always describing. I may have hidden some of the feelings, but having had a child at that time would have been so much worse for me. I was certainly scared, and it's not something you want necessarily to do, but I don't see it in that whole ethical or moral framework. I guess I really don't think of the fetus as a child until it is really a child.

But you'll hear plenty of abortion stories. I will tell you what happened next after that was over, which is what I really want to talk about. I became pregnant again a couple of years later. I wanted to have the child, but my husband didn't. It was very hard; I didn't know what to do. I was kind of in despair.

I got three or four addresses, again from women in the park.

My husband wasn't going to come with me. Partly I didn't want him to come; I probably was mad at him. I had this good friend, and she said, "You're not going by yourself." I was very grateful to her. She said, "I'll go with you," and she did.

I remember very clearly traveling to those places—to the end of Long Island and the end of Queens and the end of Brooklyn. I went to each one of these guys, but they wouldn't do it. One guy said, "Look, if you weren't married, I would risk it, but you're married and maybe you just have to make do." He felt I didn't need an abortion that much. I'll never forget. The only person we could find was some distance away and didn't sound very good to me at all. I was very frightened . . . terribly frightened.

Shortly after that, I remember, it was a freezing night, I was visiting people, and I ran home very fast. I was distraught and terrified because I was going to have to go either to Puerto Rico or someplace else. It was late in the pregnancy; it could almost have been the second trimester. That night I ran home at top speed—I can't tell you—in the cold, crying, from about eight blocks away. I ran all the way home and just fell into bed. I remember I had a terrible bellyache from the running.

When I woke up the next morning, I was bleeding fiercely. It seemed to me I was having a miscarriage. I'd had another miscarriage, and both my children were born early, so it was not a weird thing that this would happen to me.

So I called this doctor I'd been to several times before, and he said to me, "Did you do something?" I said, "No! It's just like the last time I had a miscarriage. I'm bleeding." And he said, "Call somebody in your family. Get some ergot [a drug that stops uterine contractions]." I said, "Don't you want me to come over?" and he said, *"No! Don't come."*

By this time my father had had heart attacks, so I didn't tell him anything about it. I continued to bleed. I bled and bled, for days. I was really in terrible shape, and I couldn't get anyone to take care of me. On about the third or fourth day, my doctor finally said, "Come over." He had to do a D&C.

Sometime after that, when I spoke to my father about it, he said: "That doctor was being watched. There's no other explanation. He was a kind guy. He knew you. He must have recently done something, and he was scared."

These things are not talked about a lot, this kind of criminalization of the medical profession, the danger these doctors were in. It meant that they could not take care of you. It's not even about abortion.

A good friend had an even clearer experience with this. She also was bleeding at the wrong time, and it didn't stop. She went to the emergency room here at a Catholic hospital, and they refused to take care of her. They just flatly refused. They said she had to have a rabbit test to see if she was pregnant, and the results would take a couple of days. They would not touch her because she *might* be pregnant, and they *might* disturb the child. She continued to bleed, and they would not take care of her. She was a little skinny woman; she didn't have that much blood. Well, she wasn't pregnant. It turned out she had a tumor. It was an emergency—she had to be operated on immediately.

Your life, a woman's life, was simply not the first thing that they had on their minds at all. Not only that: Even if the doctor had compassion—and in my friend's case, one of the doctors was very anxious about her—they couldn't do anything unless they were willing to risk a great deal.

I think women died all the time when abortions were illegal. The horrible abortions were one way; the other way was the refusal of institutions—medical, church, and state—to care for you, their willingness to let you die.

It's important to be public about the issue, and I have been for years. I helped organize one of the first abortion speak-outs in the country, which was held at the Washington Square Methodist Church in New York City back in the late sixties.

But I'll be very truthful. I never liked the slogan "Abortion on Demand," and most of my friends hated it. We'd go on marches, and we could never say it. It's such a trivialization of the experience. It's like "Toothpaste on Demand." If somebody said there should be birth control on demand, I would say yes. That would make a lot of sense. If I ask for a diaphragm, if I ask for a condom, I should just get it right off the bat.

But an abortion . . . After all, it's a surgical procedure and really a very serious thing to undertake. It's not a small matter. Just because I didn't suffer a lot around my abortion, suffering is not the only thing that makes something important. I didn't suffer, but it was important. And when you say "on demand," it ignores the real question, which is: Where are you in your pregnancy? If you're in the sixth month, it's probably not wise, not good for you. Not that I think if a woman goes to a clinic and wants to have an abortion, she shouldn't have it when she needs it. It's just that there's a lot of stuff to think about.

The last demonstration I went to was in Montpelier, Vermont [Mobilization for Women's Lives, November 12, 1989]. There were about twenty-five hundred women and men. The governor spoke, a woman governor, Madeline Kunin; and, one of the great highlights, an older woman—older than me, even (I'm sixty-seven)—from Catholics for a Free Choice spoke wonderfully; and I spoke.

I said that abortion is only the tip of the iceberg. These guys who run at the clinics—and by the way, our Burlington clinic was really raided, with people knocked down—are point men who make the noise and false hypocritical statements about human life, which they don't much care about, really. What they really want to do is take back ownership of women's bodies. They want to return us to a time when even our children weren't our own; we were simply the receptacles to have these children. The great novels of the nineteenth and early twentieth centuries were often about women who knew that if they took one wrong step, their children would be taken from them.

And another point I made is that abortion isn't what they're thinking about; they're really thinking about sex. They're really thinking about love and reducing it to its most mechanical aspects—that is to say, the mechanical fact of intercourse as a specific act to make children in this world, and thinking of its use in any other way as wrong and wicked. They are determined to reduce women's normal sexual responses, to end them, really, when we've just had a couple of decades of admitting them.

My generation—and only in our later years—and the one right after mine have been the only ones to really enjoy any sexual freedom. The kids have to know that it's not just the right to abortion which is essential; it's their right to a sexual life.

Elizabeth Janeway

This native of Brooklyn Heights, born in 1913, is a novelist, essayist, and reviewer; she is also a past president of the Author's Guild and former chair of the New York Council for the Humanities. Among Janeway's books, all concerned with the status of women, are *Powers of the Weak*, *Improper Behavior*, *Between Myth and Morning*, *Women Awakening* and *Man's World, Woman's Place*; she is currently writing a book about aging.

Married for over fifty years to economist Eliot Janeway, Elizabeth has two sons, two grandsons, and a granddaughter.

I was twenty-one and living in New York when I got pregnant. The man I was in a relationship with was Eliot, whom I later married. I was in my senior year at Barnard, which must have been 1935. It happened after I took a year off from school.

The year I dropped out of college, I worked. The reason was money. Nineteen thirty-three was the Depression year. My father was a naval architect, and nobody wanted a yacht. And the Navy Department—this was pre–Defense Department—wasn't ordering any destroyers in 1933, so there wasn't an awful lot of money around.

During that year, I wrote advertising copy for the basement of A&S [Abraham & Straus, a department store]. The job kept me in food, clothes, and made me some interesting friends. It was a very interesting time and experience altogether. I've always been happy that I did it.

When I managed to get back to college in the fall of '34, I may have been one of the first persons aided by the federal government. The New Deal was getting under way, and there was something called FERA, which was Federal Emergency Relief Assistance. A part of it was aimed at college students. For twenty dollars a month, you put in so many hours of time working for something that was designated by the college, and what I did was copy things for a history professor. There weren't any photocopiers, so I went to the Columbia University library and copied Italian longhand, although I couldn't read Italian. That paid my subway fare from home, ten cents each way, and lunch for forty-five cents.

By the time I returned to college, Eliot had graduated. He'd been abroad and done some work at the London School of Economics with one of the great names. He didn't get a graduate degree. Things began to kind of go bad, and he came back. I had met him once years before, but we met again in a typical situation—at a party at the house of a mutual friend.

Sex before marriage was common at that time in New York among people who were—I don't know whether I should say . . . avant-garde, I suppose, to a degree—students at Barnard, yes. I would certainly say there was nothing particularly out of the way about that. Among my friends, having sex before marriage was acceptable, and having an abortion was acceptable . . . yes indeed, you would have been an idiot if you were pregnant and not married and didn't have an abortion—unless you truly wanted that child.

In the thirties, the immorality was if you got pregnant . . . it wasn't if you had an abortion. You were pretty damned immoral if you went and got yourself—as they used to say—knocked up, but if you did, your family, if no one else, could be involved to see that you got taken care of. I think a lot of doctors across the country were willing to see that . . . at the upper levels . . . you got looked after. At the time, too, abortion was not much talked about, and certainly the Catholic church was not as powerful at the publicity level as it is today.

I didn't go to my parents, but my sister helped me with money. She was ten years older than I and had been very much an adult to me when I was little. She immediately gave me what she could, and it was what was needed. As for my parents, my mother and father were in some of their ways Victorian, though not in their minds, if you see what I mean. They were both open-minded about all kinds of ideas, about culture, but one didn't sit down and have a chat with them about what should you know about sex.

At the time I got pregnant, Eliot and I didn't have any money between us. He was doing various bits of writing around on economics or one thing or another, but he didn't have a steady job and was as broke as I was. I decided to have an abortion because there was no other thing to do. It would have been totally impossible to raise a child. It seems to me that when people talk about abortions—certainly, the right-to-lifers—it's put in the context that you don't want to be inconvenienced for nine months. Well, that's not what you base your decision on at all. Once you have a child, you have it. What I was thinking about was, can I raise this child responsibly for twenty years after it is born? It was clearly a ridiculous proposition for us.

The actual abortion was comfortable, clean, the absolute tops. That was because the surgeon who did it was a trained, skilled, very pleasant person who certainly should have had a brilliant career anywhere, but he was Jewish and so had been exiled from

Hitler's Germany. I didn't have a horror story, but certainly the doctor who worked on me must have had a terrible story. It was his horror story.

The gynecologist whom I had seen—who told me I was pregnant—had come from Vienna and kept up a connection with some of the German doctors. He referred me to this man. I went to an apartment here in Manhattan, somewhere uptown, and there was an apparatus set up. I don't think I was scared; I felt that this would be like minor surgery. It was not terribly painful—I was early on—and not terribly pleasant either. The doctor very sweetly said, "Would you like a little brandy?" and I certainly did. I paid him, I think, one hundred dollars. Both doctors were quite sympathetic.

I fitted into one of those funny little loopholes of time where you could be sure that a good doctor who knew about cleanliness and so on was operating. The kind of concern about whether the abortion was safe—physically or anything like that—which certainly must have been painfully in people's minds in the fifties and sixties, was just absent when I went through the looking glass.

It's very possible my experience was rare. It depended on the fact that the gynecologist I went to had come from Vienna at a time when he could be absorbed into the American Medical Association without any problems. It was because of the Depression coinciding with the Hitler terror that the German doctors who came over later—who were as well trained, no doubt, as my gynecologist—ran into the American doctors here saying, "We're not going to let you in. You're going to take our trade away." So the new German doctors simply kept themselves as best they could, waiting for the New York State Academy to certify them. It was known that some of these doctors did abortions . . . at least, I was sent to one by my gynecologist.

The fact that abortion was illegal never bothered me at all. But remember, we were the generation that had grown up under

Prohibition, and anytime we had a drink, we were doing something illegal. I suppose I'd say that the Depression years and the Roosevelt years were such a change that, if you were part of that generation, you were more than ready to challenge old ideas. It was all part of the time—the people begging on the streets, selling apples, people who had had decent jobs. It was a terrible time. Many of us who were young then were in a kind of basic rebellion against doing things the company way.

If there was activism around abortion, it was merged into a kind of left-wingism. We just figured that the thing to do was to liberalize the whole society. There was very little separation of the issue or logical thinking about it. I don't think we even imagined then that abortion could become legal.

We certainly believed in birth control. You do remember how restrictive the laws were then; there had been laws in Connecticut and Massachusetts against using contraceptives, people blithely stamping into a person's private life. But in the thirties, you could go to Margaret Sanger's clinic down on Sixteenth Street and get birth control. After my abortion, in fact, I did. You didn't have to go through lines of anybody saying, "Don't do that." You made an appointment, you went down, they fitted you with a pessary . . . diaphragm, and you used it.

Eliot and I finally got married when we had enough money to feel that it was okay to have children; we did that along about 1938. In fact, five years later we had a child whom we raised, then we had another, then I lost a third. That experience was infinitely more painful than the abortion. I carried the child to term and lost it at birth. It was a bad pregnancy, so I suppose you could have predicted that that would happen, but I tried not to think ahead.

The abortion I simply took in stride. It was a necessary thing to do. I suppose I felt the saddest about the abortion when my children grew up, and I knew how much I loved them and how great they were, and I regretted not having that child. But I think our decision was right. There was no way we could have raised that child, and as soon as we could raise a child, we did.

The abortion didn't seem to have any particular pall of something that had to be secret or that was shameful, and it has not been at all hard to talk about publicly. When I signed the *Ms.* magazine petition in 1972 with other women who had had abortions, the only thing I really remember is that Barbara Tuchman [the late historian] did, too. We both laughed together about doing it. I said, "Barbara, we're the same age, almost"— she was a little bit older. "I certainly felt like the oldest elephant doing this and I was so glad to find you." She felt the same way.

K a y   B o y l e

Kay Boyle, a passionate and prolific writer whose work reflects the tumultuous periods through which she has lived, has written forty books, among them the novels *Year Before Last*, *The Underground Woman*, and *Death of a Man*; a recent poetry collection, *This Is Not A Letter*; a book of essays, *Words That Must Somehow Be Said*; and her autobiography, *Being Geniuses Together*, written with Robert McAlmon. She twice received the O. Henry Award for the year's best short story.

Born in 1902, Boyle moved to Europe in the late twenties, where she eventually joined the expatriate generation in Paris, counting Samuel Beckett and Marcel Duchamp among her closest friends. Married three times, Boyle raised six children and two stepchildren. Today, she is a grandmother of seventeen, great-grandmother of six, and resides in the Redwoods Retirement Home in Mill Valley, California.

There were two abortions—one in New York and one in Paris. The first, in New York, was in 1921, when I was nineteen years old. My husband and I lived in a shabby furnished room on East Fifteenth Street—I can see it so well now in every detail. We had that one room and a bathroom, where we cooked our meals; the carpeting in the hall, on the stairs, and in our room was alive with fleas; and the walls and ceilings crawled with spiders. I had a job as secretary in the New York office of *Broom* magazine, a great, big, beautiful art magazine that was published in Italy, and my husband, who had been a French exchange student in Cincinnati in the four years I had known him, had earned a degree in electrical engineering at the university there. But when he followed me to New York, where we were married, the only job he could get was reading meters for the gas and electric company in New York City.

I don't recall having access myself to birth control measures, but my French husband used condoms. I believe it was my sister who told me about the doctor I went to when I became pregnant. She was a wonderful woman, Dr. Mary Halton, who specialized in abortions for working women. What was very moving were the other women in Dr. Halton's waiting room, very young and very worried-looking, some of them with two or three children already, and some of them having abortions without their husbands' knowledge. But for me, having an abortion wasn't for a moment an anguished decision. My husband and I were both working very hard, but we were poor and realized we couldn't afford a baby. I never thought of the illegality of abortion. I just knew it was the only thing to do at that particular time.

Dr. Halton's method of abortion stretched over five or six visits. After a preliminary interview with her, a future date was set when you would climb on the operating table, and she would start the process of gradually penetrating the womb. [Dilation of the cervix was either a prelude to a D&C or used to stimulate labor.] It was a quite painful procedure as Dr. Halton was not prepared to anesthetize her patients; at times, sitting in the waiting room, one could hear the screams of a woman from behind the closed doors. She told me, "The important thing is, when you go home, if you feel something pushing to come out, or if you start bleeding, you must call me at once, any time of the night or day." One night, I felt this coming, so I rushed to the toilet and the fetus came out. My husband was there with me and he telephoned Dr. Halton. She came . . . I think it was twelve o'clock at night . . . and saw that everything was as it should be.

I was thinking yesterday how clearly I remember the passing of the little thing. I didn't feel guilty. I wasn't scared. You can't be scared of a reality; you have to accept it, face it, summon a bit more courage than you previously had.

Of course, it was not public knowledge that Dr. Mary Halton was performing abortions. She was known professionally for bringing babies into the world. I was never worried that she might be arrested, for I was sure she had taken all the necessary precautions. I had no sense at all of anything precarious taking place. Dr. Halton's mere presence reassured one.

About a year later, my husband and I went to Europe on borrowed money. I had my first child in France, in 1927, after separating from my husband. The father was Ernest Walsh, a poet and publisher, who had been an aviator in the First World War and had a crash which smashed his lungs. He was very ill with tuberculosis and died before my daughter was born.

I had that baby because I wanted Ernest Walsh's child. I didn't actually know I was going to become pregnant, but that was the very deep feeling within me at the time. I felt no guilt about having a baby out of wedlock, no shame . . . oh, no, for heaven's sake . . . of course not. I didn't think that anyone with any intelligence respected such arbitrary laws as marriage and divorce, and certainly not in artistic circles.

I didn't have much money, so I joined the Raymond Duncan Colony, where my daughter would be taken care of all day while I took care of one of the two shops run by Raymond Duncan in downtown Paris. Raymond Duncan was Isadora's brother. I don't know if it was an "artists' colony," but it was a mess, whatever it was. Raymond Duncan himself was rather pathetic, but the woman who lived there with him was a very bossy woman. She said that once I had brought my child to the colony, she became one of the family of the fifteen children there. I no longer had any rights as a mother, she told me, which I suppose is the rule of a colony, but I was brokenhearted.

In the summer, Raymond Duncan and the lady he lived with took all the children to the south of France, where they had a second location. I was left behind to work at the Duncan shop on the Boulevard Saint-Germain to keep the shop open. That was the first time I had been separated from my daughter and I went completely mad. It was the only time in my life I've ever been promiscuous. Some people believe I was a very wild woman when I was young and had a lot of love affairs, but I wasn't and I didn't. When I got pregnant that summer, I had no idea who the father was.

I was great friends then with Harry and Caresse Crosby. They were writers and publishers of the Black Sun Press and later published my first book of short stories. I told Caresse I had to have an abortion, and she and I went to various midwives, but we couldn't find a single midwife in Paris who would do an abortion. One lady said, *"Je ne manges pas de ce pain,"* which means "I do not eat that kind of bread." We eventually found a very expensive procedure; the Crosbys were rich, and it wasn't a problem for them to put me up in a beautiful hospital.

What I remember so well is the night before I was to have the abortion. I was in a room in the hospital, and there were babies, babies, babies crying everywhere. The nurse on that floor had too much work to do. She couldn't run fast enough to this baby and then to that baby. So about midnight, I said, "Give me some of the babies." She brought me *four*. I had two in the curve of one arm as I lay in bed, and two in the curve of my other arm, and I was able to soothe them. Such a peculiar situation the night before an abortion! I was operated on in the morning, under an anesthetic, while a gentle nurse held my hand.

The extraordinary thing about my story is that Dr. Mary Halton was the doctor who brought two of my children into the world twenty years later. I was in Europe for almost twenty years because I never had the money to come back. I finally came back in 1941; married my third husband, an Austrian, a wonderful man; and we had two children, a daughter and a son.

It must have been my sister who put me in touch with Dr. Halton again. It was very strange—Dr. Halton remembered me; I don't know how she did, but she did. The birth went splendidly with my daughter, Faith, but eleven months later, when it was Ian's turn to come, that was difficult.

I was living in Mount Vernon, and my brother-in-law brought me into the city that night because the pains had begun. Dr. Halton came to the hospital right away, and things weren't going very well. It was terribly slow. And then they discovered that Ian had turned himself around the wrong way. I could see that Dr. Halton was worried. She had a bandage on one hand, which she said she had cut, and, because of that, didn't feel she could handle the birth. There was a young woman expecting a baby there that night, and she had brought her doctor, a great expert, to the hospital. He was the one who came in and took Ian out with forceps.

You ask whether I worried before or after about my decisions to have these two abortions. I don't know if it's a virtue or a vice, but when I come to a decision—a decision based on reality, which in the case of my two abortions was that I did not have the money to support a family—I do not for a moment torture myself with misgivings as to whether or not I have done the right thing. It was the only thing to do.

I am very family oriented, though I never thought about wanting a large family. When reality is there, one accepts reality. Through the years, people would ask me after a lecture or an interview how I managed to have six children and bring up two stepchildren, and yet write forty books. I would always give a stupid, sanctimonious answer, saying, "It takes infinite patience and infinite love." Do you know what Grace Paley says when she is asked the same question? She says, "I neglected them." So I said, "Grace, may I say that?" And she said, "Absolutely." So now I say that too.

P o l l y   B e r g e n

Polly Bergen, born in 1930 in Knoxville, Tennessee, began her career singing on her own radio show at the age of thirteen, then went on to become a stage, screen, and television actress. She received an Emmy for her performance in *The Helen Morgan Story,* Emmy nominations for *War and Remembrance* and the *The Winds of War,* and a Golden Globe Award for *The Caretakers.* Also a successful businesswoman, Bergen was the first woman appointed to the Singer Company's board in its 124-year history.

Three times married, Bergen, who lives in Beverly Hills, is mother of three—two adopted children, Peter and Pamela Kerry (better known as "PK"), and a stepdaughter, Kathy; she is also grandmother of three. In recognition of those achievements, Bergen has received the National Mothers' Day Committee's Outstanding Mother Award.

When I got my menstrual period, I thought I'd hurt myself—I had no idea what had happened. My mother found some old rags that I had thrown away, literally dirty old dishrags. . . . My mother and father were very stoic people, and father always said, "Big girls don't cry," so I never told anyone. My mother took me to the doctor, and he explained it to me.

Though my mother and father, who were Southern Baptists, were very loving and very giving, I would never have had a conversation with them about very personal things, certainly not about my menstrual period. But as a child, I also missed having really close girlfriends to talk to. From the time I was very little, we moved every three or four months. My father was a construction engineer, but I lived like an army brat. We were *always* in a new place. I learned at a very early age not to make friends because it was far too painful.

My father could not read or write; my mother went to the third grade. We were on welfare at one time when my father's scaffold gave way and he broke his back and was in a hospital for six months. My mother went to work, doing whatever job she could get. So at a very early age, I did the cooking and I did the cleaning and I did the laundry and I did the pressing and I made the meals and I went to school and I got straight A's. Then once they had my sister—she was born when I was eleven years old—I took her to nursery school and I picked her up and I took care of her and I couldn't go out because I had to watch her if my mother and father were on night shift. Childhood didn't have any reality for me. I was an adult—I had always been an adult. I don't say that for anybody to feel sorry for me; I don't think I knew I was *missing* anything.

I was always led to believe by my mother and father that I could be anything in the world I wanted to be. I knew when I was ten, eleven that I was going to be a singer and an actress. At fifteen and sixteen, I was a band singer in Las Vegas and Reno, and my mother was traveling with me as my sister. I remember saying I was twenty-two. Of course, when you are working in Vegas, and you are lying about your age, you could never let people know you didn't know everything because if you didn't then how could you be twenty-two? So I was pretending that I knew everything.

One of the things I knew nothing whatsoever about was sex. I remember in my senior year—now this sounds as though I was born in 1800, and we are in fact talking about 1947—sitting on the back stairs and having my girlfriend explain to me how you had babies. I thought if somebody touched you, you'd get pregnant. I knew really nothing because I never asked anybody. I asked her because she was somebody I had gotten moderately close to, a wonderful Italian girl who shot right through all the defenses I had.

I had sex for the first time when I was seventeen, I guess. I was in school, working at a drugstore, and there was a salesman who was there several times a week. He was extraordinarily handsome. I just thought he was the most sophisticated man . . . he was like Cary Grant to me.

We had sex in a car, and I didn't realize it until I got home and my panties were bloody. There was a moment when it was painful, but I had no idea that what had happened was that I had just had sex. We were doing a lot of heavy petting, but, you understand, I had never looked at a penis nor had I ever touched one. I had absolutely no idea that his penis was in my vagina, no idea.

When I got home, I was really devastated because I thought, How can this thing which is supposed to be so wonderful have happened, and I didn't even know? That it happened the way it did, I knew he didn't really care about me. I never saw him after the one time, and later on I discovered that he was married and had four children. I did not get pregnant.

When I was seventeen, I convinced my mom and dad that I had to move to Hollywood to get a job. I found an apartment in a court on Orange Drive. A lot of people who lived in the court were in show business. This girl moved in with me so we could share expenses.

I earned what little money I earned as a demo maker. I would walk up and down Vine Street—where all the houses that published music were—and go in and out of the publishers' offices. I don't know what they paid me—three dollars a record? Five dollars a record? I had enough money to barely pay my rent. I remember we had cases of Campbell's soup because you could get that real cheap. I could eat it three times a day; it was not a big deal. We also used hot water to make tomato soup with ketchup.

I remember once going to a party in the court. Jackie Gleason was there—he was just starting and nobody knew who he was—and there was a young man whom I fell madly in love with, head over heels in love with. We dated—in those days you *actually* dated.

There were really only two ways it was acceptable then to go to bed with someone: if you were madly in love and they had proven to you that they were madly in love with you, or if you were drunk. I really believed that I was in love with him because you certainly couldn't admit that you just wanted to go to bed with somebody; I wasn't even sure I *did.* But I thought that would make him happy. Then I would know for sure that he loved me, and then we would naturally . . . get married and have children.

I wanted to fall in love, and I wanted to get married. You were supposed to fall in love, you were supposed to get married, and you were supposed to have a family; one didn't happen without all the others. But falling in love did come second; my ambition was very, very overwhelming.

We had sex. Getting pregnant was something that never entered my mind; it was something that only happened to bad girls. I was not promiscuous. I had had sex twice, maybe three times. You never expected to have sex with someone, so it was never planned, and you weren't prepared at all.

Birth control wasn't something that I ever would have discussed. I was aware that there was such a thing as a condom, but I'd never seen one. I was not aware of diaphragms. To give you an idea of how things were then, my first job in the drugstore was to wrap Kotex boxes in brown paper . . . Kotex boxes were always wrapped in brown paper, always, always. To go in and ask for them was the most humiliating thing. Forget guys going in and asking for condoms—women felt exactly the same way going in and asking for anything having to do with the menstrual period.

The night we had sex was the last time I saw the young man. He didn't disappear—he lived in the court—but he went off on a job. I never heard from him again.

A couple months passed, and I didn't feel very well. I don't even remember how I found out I was pregnant. My roommate may have taken me to her doctor because I certainly did not have a doctor. I'd never been to a gynecologist in my life. I think the last time that anyone had looked at me from the waist down was when I thought I hurt myself when I was thirteen. Of course, we pretended I was married. The doctor said I was pregnant, and we came home, and I was hysterical. I cried for a long time.

I don't remember giving an abortion a lot of thought. That was what I had to do. I didn't know how I was going to do it, but I knew that that's what I was going to have to do. I loved this man, and I wished that I had heard from him, but I hadn't and obviously he didn't care about me as much as I cared about him . . . so I was not going to call *him*.

I was certainly not going to call my mom and my dad, because everything that they had ever thought about me would be destroyed. I was this perfect child to them. I had always done everything they wanted me to do.

I couldn't tolerate the idea that my parents would know that I had not been a "nice girl." My whole concern was that I had gone to bed with a man I was not married to. In my own mind, if people knew, I would have been a whore. There was always that one girl in school who "put out," and everybody laughed about her and jeered about her and made fun of her and she was cheap and she was bad.

I couldn't have that baby. That baby would ruin my whole life. It would ruin my mother and father; it would ruin me; it would ruin everybody who had ever known me and loved me.

It was all about the moral judgment; it had really very little to do with anything else, because I love babies. I love babies.

Everybody carried that moral judgment around—that's what we were all taught to believe was right. It makes me very angry—I have a tremendous amount of anger about it. I have a lot of anger directed at myself for being stupid and getting in that jam to begin with. I feel angry at the man. I feel angry that boys were raised to believe that the most important thing was to get some girl in bed, girls were raised to believe that the most important thing was *not* to do it, and this conditioning created so much torture and hell for everybody, for boys as well as girls.

Nobody ever took into consideration *feelings*. They never took into consideration wanting to be held or wanting to be loved or wanting to be cared for or wanting to not feel alone or frightened. I think even today there are so many young girls and so many young boys who get involved sexually because they need somebody to hold them. The girls put out . . . putting out seems like such a small price to pay for not being lonely.

My roommate knew somebody who knew somebody who knew somebody who said that they had somebody who could take care of this. I didn't have any money. I borrowed the money—about $300. In those days, if you were under contract to a studio as a starlet, you got $150 a week, so $300 was a lot of money. I was not under contract to a studio. I got part of it from my roommate and part of it from a couple of people in the court. You couldn't tell them what the money was for; you lied.

My roommate had this little old beat-up car. She had a job out of town and asked me if I wanted her to stay. She would have had to turn down a job, so I said no. I told her that I would be all right. I asked her if I could borrow the car and she said yes. By then, I would say certainly I was over three months pregnant; it could have been four.

I'd been given a name and an address. The building was in downtown Los Angeles. It was one of those little Hollywood bungalows, tiny with little stairs up to the porch. I knocked on the door. I remember vaguely that the man appeared to be Spanish . . . or Brazilian, Italian.

I was very scared, but I didn't want *him* to know. I was fearful that he would take advantage of me. I was fearful that I was alone and walking into a house where there did not appear to be anybody else. And while this man had come recommended, I mean, there wasn't any way to know. I was fearful that some-how it would make me more defenseless if he knew I was scared. I felt I had to walk in like I was this real tough cookie who knew what I was doing, with this kind of don't-fuck-with-me atti-tude—not that I would have ever said "fuck" at that time—to protect myself.

The first thing he did was ask me if I had the money. I gave him the money and he said, "Go in there and take off your clothes. You can leave your top on." The room had very funny dark green walls, peeling. There was what looked like a kitchen table with oilcloth on it and linoleum. It wasn't *in* a kitchen, but there was a shelf that had a lot of knives and whatnot on it. I really, really didn't want to see, so you just don't see . . . you don't look. I was so afraid that if I looked I would run, and I knew I could not run. I knew I had to do that . . . I knew I could *not* have that baby.

I don't remember being afraid of being hurt, afraid of it hurting. It seems to me my girlfriend had said, "Look, it's nothing. You'll go in, it'll be taken care of, it'll be over, and your life will be all right again." I went in thinking that was the way it was going to be, and of course, it was extremely painful.

I went into the room, and there was a sheet lying there, which I wrapped around myself. He came in and said, "Get on the table." I haven't any idea what he did; I didn't see anything. I know he used something very sharp—it was a very, very sharp thing. I didn't make any noise at all. I bit through my lip. I tried not to cry; I didn't want him to see me cry.

He really wasn't a terrible person. I was very lucky. He didn't grab me; he didn't do anything that was remotely sexual. Whatever he did, he did. He finished doing it, started to walk out of the room, and said, "You can get dressed now. Wear something, you're going to have some bleeding. Go home and lie down. You'll have a few cramps, like a bad period, but you should be fine." I said, "Is it all done?" He said, "Yeah, it's all done." I said, "Thanks a lot," and I got up and got dressed, and walked out.

I got into the car. I wanted desperately to get away from the house, but I was shaking so hard at first I couldn't get the key in the ignition. I finally got the car started, drove half a block, turned a corner, and parked. I guess I cried for about an hour. Then I fixed my makeup in the car and went home. I had to say hello to everybody as I was walking through the courtyard; they were all sitting on their little doorsteps and talking and laughing.

Three days later my girlfriend came home. I had managed to get up a couple of times and make some soup. Blood was on the bed; it was on the floor; it was on the carpet. We had run out of sheets and the mattress was ruined. I guess I did think I was dying. The doctor said I was dying because I had lost a lot of blood by the time my roommate got me to see him. But you know, I'm sure there was a part of me that thought I was supposed to die. I had done this terrible thing—I had had sex and I'd gotten pregnant. The abortion added to it, but that was not the terrible thing.

After my abortion, I ended up falling in love and marrying my roommate's brother, who was a very successful actor. He wasn't involved in any of it; he thought he'd married a virgin. During our marriage, which lasted about five years, I don't think either one of us ever really thought about children. But when that marriage was over, I remarried a year later, and I desperately wanted to have children. I was twenty-five.

In my first and then in my second marriage, I'd had a number of what appeared to be miscarriages—some that resulted in D&Cs. They were devastating because I really desperately, desperately wanted a child. Those miscarriages always reminded me of the abortion. I had *such guilt*—guilt about what the abortion had done, what the abortion had left. Also, I remember that, as the fairy tale goes, you fall in love, you get married, and you have children; those are the three things that make you this perfect person. I couldn't seem to get the last one right.

I finally went to a fertility-sterility expert in New York. During the period that followed, I had three ectopic pregnancies. With the first one, it exploded, and they rushed me to the hospital. They did not know I was pregnant, so they obviously did not know I had a tubular pregnancy. It was a great stroke of luck that a doctor who had never seen me considered that possibility. I almost died by the time they found out what it was, I had lost so much blood.

At that time they had created a new procedure whereby they could reconstruct the fallopian tube, and my gynecologist did that. I then went through about a year of the single most excruciating, terrible tests in the entire world . . . they literally force air into the tube. I went through that until they were fairly sure that the tube was functioning properly. By then I was twenty-seven, because I adopted my first child, PK, that year, which was 1957.

Two years later I was doing a Broadway show, and I started having pains very similar to the pains I had had during the first tubular pregnancy. Up until then there was no test that they could give you to detect tubular pregnancies; you found out when you blew up. I went in, and they did the exploratory test. It was tubular again, in the reconstructed tube. They discovered it before it blew up.

When he finished, my gynecologist told me, "Somebody did a terrible thing to you. . . . I have never seen such a mess. It's extraordinary. You are totally full of scar tissue, as though someone had taken some kind of sharp instrument and just gone through everything. The miracle is that you got pregnant at all." He cleared out the tube that had been totally closed with scar tissue, and reconstructed the other.

I adopted my second baby in 1959—a boy, Peter; we moved out to California; and in 1962 I got pregnant again. It was a tubular pregnancy that nobody diagnosed. I blew up, and they took everything out. I was thirty-three.

Nobody knew through the years about my abortion except my one girlfriend. About a week before the pro-choice march on Washington in 1989 was the first time I spoke about it . . . at a breakfast for mothers and daughters. I spoke out because I suddenly realized that there was a possibility that what I had lived with would happen again.

Part of my decision was related to the sense I always had of being a failure. Because I did what I did the way I did it, having that abortion, I left myself unable to do that which I wanted to do so badly, which was to deliver a child. I realized that could happen to millions and millions of other women—that is, if they didn't die.

Beyond that, I don't believe that anyone has the right to tell a woman that she must have an abortion, and I don't think it's right for anyone to tell a woman that she cannot have one. Once I allow a politician to do that, I am not only losing my battle, but I am losing the pro-lifer's battle as well. Once you allow politicians to tell you you can't have one, those same politicians can turn around and say you must have one, or it can only be a boy, it can only have blue eyes, it can only be a girl, you can only have two, you can't have any.

The longing to have children really ended a long time ago for me, when I had children of my own. I always referred to PK as my daughter, Peter as my son. I never referred to Kathy as my stepdaughter. They are my children. But there was always a part of me that regretted not having had the experience of actually carrying and delivering a child. The thing that finally got me past it was being with PK when she gave birth to Zachary, my second grandchild.

I was her substitute Lamaze partner in case her husband, Scott, fainted or couldn't show up. I had flown out here and gone to all the classes. We had done this whole thing together, and it was going to be great. So she starts labor, and it's a very mild labor. She was terrifically funny . . . she was King Kong, the biggest pregnant woman I've ever seen in my life. We go to Santa Monica to this wonderful women's clinic. Scott was there, and we're all suited up, wearing our green and our masks, with our booties on.

Now they start doing monitoring after like eight hours. She's not going into full labor, and the baby is starting to show stress. They finally decide to do a C-section, and Scott and I both say, "Can't we be there?" and they say, "Sure, of course, you can be there."

So I'm standing behind her and I'm talking and I'm wiping the sweat off. She had one of those blocks [lower body anesthesia], so she's wide awake and she's talking. I can see over the sheet. If I stand really on tiptoes, I can see everything. I replaced Barbara Walters on a show called "Not for Women Only," and I was for several shows in operating rooms and watched surgery. I'm very strong about that kind of thing. Sometimes I will either throw up or pass out later on, but in emergencies, you want somebody, call me.

Now I start to get fascinated because here is my daughter, she's lying here and she's talking to her husband and she's feeling nothing, and they're going, "Eeeh!" And then they're going, "Aaah!" And they got a clamp here, and they got a clamp here, and they got a clamp there, and there's this gigantic hole I'm looking at and really basically no blood.

So this young woman doctor puts her hands into this hole, and all of a sudden I see this head come up . . . I see the top of the head, and then I see the whole head, and then I see her turn the baby—because he was so fucking big—so she could get the shoulders out without breaking any ribs. They pulled this baby out, and I saw it, I saw it, I saw it! It was a ten-pound baby . . . this was *not* one of those little scrawly babies. It was a grown-up kid! I yelled, "It's a boy!"

That did it for me . . . that did it, that did it. Oh, what an experience that was. . . .

Jim   Friedl

A retired marine master sergeant and veteran of World War II, Korea, and Vietnam, sixty-seven-year-old Jim Friedl is new to the dialogue about abortion and choice. He has known since he was a young man that his mother, Ruth Irene Friedl, died at the age of twenty-seven, in 1929, from an illegal abortion. But it was only three years ago, in response to the growing threat to choice, that he and his sister, Virginia Hall, a retired nurse, began to speak publicly about their loss. In 1990, Friedl testified before a Senate committee in support of the proposed Freedom of Choice Act, originally introduced by Senators Bob Packwood and Alan Cranston, that would guarantee legislatively the right to abortion given to women by the Supreme Court in *Roe* v. *Wade*.

Friedl, father of six, lives with his second wife, Vera, in Concord, California.

You see that dining room table there? My earliest recollection is of my father standing at the head of the table. I must have been four years old; my sister was two. See this picture here? That's exactly the way he was dressed—same suit and everything. I can still see him standing there, and a woman in a dress on the floor. All I can see is her hair . . . I can't see her face. That was my mother's death scene. My father didn't know what happened. He had no idea. She hadn't told him she was pregnant.

At the time my mother died, which was 1929, my dad was

an up-and-coming young businessman; they lived in a nice, big, rented home right near the Denver city limits. He had started at the age of twelve as an office boy in a wholesale grocery company, J. S. Brown Mercantile. My mother was a housewife.

They were certainly far better off as adults than they were when they were growing up, but they were heavily in debt, I guess because he wanted to give my mother everything he could. They had new furniture. They had a telephone before either one of my grandmothers had one. One reason my mother didn't tell my father that she was pregnant was probably that she was worried about the expense of having another baby. She probably had some naive hope that the abortion could be performed but he would never find out. There's also the fact that my mother had been told after we were born that she shouldn't have any more children.

When my mother became aware that she was pregnant, she called my Aunt Alice, my father's oldest sister, long-distance, from Colorado to Idaho, which was like calling transatlantic now.

Aunt Alice had met and married a doctor from New York who'd trained at Bellevue. Evidently his parents had enough money to help him through, but without a lot of money to set up a private practice, you looked for something else. So he became the doctor for the railroad workers.

They lived in a tiny town called Mackay, in Idaho—650 people *now*. He was the only doctor in that community, and there was no hospital, no clinic, no nothing. So besides the railroad workers, he took care of all the people in the country-side—the sheepherders and farmers and miners and ranchers, most of them immigrants from the Slovenian countries. He had his clinic in the back of a drugstore and did everything for those people up there because there was nobody else.

My mother wanted my aunt to talk to Uncle Doc, but Aunt Alice told my mother there was no way he would perform an abortion. She said if he did something like that, he could lose his license. And as far as I know, that was the end of the conversation. What hurts me the most is my belief that if my mother had been able to talk to Uncle Doc herself, if she had had any way to ask him personally, he never would have turned her down. Knowing what Uncle Doc did for others, I just can't believe he would have said no.

As children, we were led to believe that my mother died of ptomaine poisoning. You see, her family had a little place outside of Denver, what we might call a truck farm. They grew their own things, but didn't know all that much about canning properly, so ptomaine poisoning was a likely candidate. I think it was my mother's family that allowed us to grow up thinking she died of ptomaine poisoning, but no one in my father's family did anything to enlighten us. That was a socially acceptable way to die, wasn't it?

I first learned that my mother died of an illegal abortion from my Aunt Alice when I was twenty-one and on active duty in the Marine Corps. I was shocked. This wasn't the kind of thing people did. That was the 1940s, and it was still a criminal act. If you found out that somebody had an abortion, it was because they weren't able to hide it, and the feeling was, shame on them. I felt ashamed that I didn't know of anybody else who'd had an abortion.

At that point, that's all I knew. It wasn't until two years ago, when my sister and I got a copy of my mother's death certificate, that we found out she died from an overdose of ergot to produce an abortion. To this day, ergot is a controlled substance. [The drug contracts the uterus and is sometimes used after childbirth; like other drugs, it is potentially fatal in large doses.] We don't know how she got the drug, but I'm sure my mother thought, If one teaspoon is good, maybe four teaspoons is great. She was an unsophisticated girl . . . I don't think she was a high school graduate . . . and I can say that she was very, very desperate.

Finding out that my mother died of an illegal abortion from a drug someone gave her made me even more furious. I felt that the people who caused deaths like my mother's ought to be in jail. The hell with jail; the death sentence was too damn good for them. That was an instinctive feeling . . . I couldn't have articulated it then. But today, absolutely, I'm glad abortion is legal. If my mother were here today and going through the same thing, she could have a safe abortion. The very fact that my father wasn't aware that she was pregnant tells us that she had to be in a very early stage of pregnancy, right? Under the same set of circumstances today, my mother would have lived.

After my mother's death, my father couldn't maintain the house. Almost immediately, we went to live with my grandparents—my father's parents—in Denver. We left our house on the outskirts and moved closer to the heart of the city.

I don't know how long after, my Dad started going out. I look back and realize that he was weighted down with grief, almost bankrupt . . . what the hell was he going to do from day to day, minute to minute? But that was a traumatic thing for me. From the bedroom assigned to me in my grandmother's house, I could see the lights of downtown Denver, way over the bridge . . . seven, eight, ten miles away. What comes back to me is just sitting there looking out at the black city trying to figure out where my dad was.

Another thing I remember was being very close to my cousins and their mother, who was my mother's sister. I used to go and visit them all the time. The thing that got me was how close they were. I used to think, Why me? Why don't I have something like this?

What makes me angriest about what happened to me is that everybody ignores the orphans. They don't even try to figure out how many children are orphaned by abortion, neither side, pro-life or pro-choice, not even a wild guess. Yet, you've got to think that, while we're sitting here right now, today, there's some four-year-old child like me out there, and the same damn thing is happening to him or her.

When we get into it now, it's not so hard to talk about, but something will hit me and I get so emotional. I can't believe how strongly I feel. After all, I don't need my mother anymore. It catches me off guard, you know, completely unaware. It just tears me up. It never ceases to amaze me that, when you talk about certain aspects of it, bang! It hits me. I'm not able to control it. But I'm sixty-six and a retired marine . . . I don't have to control anymore.

Rita Moreno

Rita Moreno, sixty, was born in Humacao, Puerto Rico. She came with her mother to New York City by boat at the age of five and began in show business the following year. The Guinness Book of World Records lists her as the first performer to win four of the entertainment industry's highest awards: an Oscar for her performance in *West Side Story*, the first Hispanic woman ever cited for that tribute; a Tony for her rendition of Googie Gomez in the Broadway comedy *The Ritz*; a Grammy for her contribution to the sound track album of the children's television series *The Electric Company*; and two Emmy awards for guest performances on *The Muppet Show* and *The Rockford Files*.

Today, Moreno has taken her one-woman concert on the road and released an exercise video for the rest of us called *Now You Can*, with an ego-boosting "it's okay not to be perfect" philosophy. She lives with husband Leonard Gordon, M.D., a retired cardiologist, in Los Angeles. They have one daughter.

When I grew up, there were very definitely good girls and bad girls. Bad girls did bad things, and sex was certainly a very bad thing.

I came to New York City from Puerto Rico and was raised a typical Catholic. I had to go to catechism, have my communion, go to confession, the whole business . . . and there was *loads* of guilt, by the pound. My mother took me to church for a while, but then she stopped going and I just went on my own because I was supposed to.

I didn't know what sex actually was, except those yearnings

41

one felt between one's legs. When I was fifteen or sixteen—this was in the forties—my mother, being very advanced for that time, gave me a book called *Being Born*. Somebody must have been talking to her, or I might have been asking an awful lot of questions. It was the strangest book I've ever read. It was an agricultural thing about seeds and trees growing and walnuts and pecans and God knows what all else. There were drawings of fallopian tubes, but, you know, what's a fallopian tube? There were only drawings of people's insides, so I had no idea how they did it, what they did. If you had said to me, "Well the man puts the penis in the woman's ear, and the baby comes out of the nose," I'd have said, "Right! Boy, that must be painful." I knew nothing, absolutely nothing.

If there were young single Latina women getting pregnant and having babies, I never heard about them because my mother wouldn't let me know about such things in those days. When Rosita was asleep—I was Rosita—then the family discussed such things, but they never talked about them in front of their kid. If I ever heard the subject discussed, it was in the most hushed tones, and *that girl got married.*

When you got your period, that's when you became a señorita; that's how it still is in Latin cultures. You know the whole thing with Jews and the bar mitzvah—"Today I am a man"? It's the same thing—big, big deals. With becoming a señorita came all the ensuing responsibilities of being a good girl and getting married soon and having lots of babies and being good to your husband.

I got married when I was thirty-four and had my daughter when I was thirty-five. I'll tell you what I think kept me from giving in to the cultural pressure to marry early and have lots of babies: just looking at my mother's life. I think it was as simple as that.

My mother divorced my father and came to New York City by herself. She was a big seventeen or eighteen years old and didn't know a word of English. She was so brave, you can't imagine. She found a job doing piecework in a factory as a seamstress and made enough money in a year's time to go back and get me.

I think my mother could have been a very successful designer, a wonderful dressmaker. But I saw a woman who sacrificed her entire life, all of her yearnings—God, it's very sad, all of her needs—for a number of men in her life. My mother believed that one didn't fool around with men, one married them; as a result she was married five times. I think my mother yearned for some kind of position in life other than the woman who scrubbed the floors, washed the dishes, and stuck a thermometer in my bottom. She gave up a lifetime for me and my various fathers.

And I saw that I had so many daddies who left. It's no accident that I would never, never have married a Latino man. I perceived them as people who left you, who abandoned you. I didn't want what happened to my mother to happen to me. Obviously the way to avoid that was not to marry and not to have children—those things went hand in hand.

I had my very first date when I was seventeen years old. I might have dated earlier, but the one time I was asked to a prom, I was working and couldn't go. In fact, I remember going to two parties in my whole teenagehood. I started working very young. When I was six years old, I'd perform at bar mitzvahs and weddings. Yes, my mother was influential, but I want to be very delicate about this because what she did she did out of ignorance, not out of any overly ambitious motives. My mother was a baby when she had me; she might have been sixteen. What did she know? The reason I was allowed to be in show business at that early age was because my mother felt that America was the land of opportunity where "my little girl could have more than I ever did." Indeed, it turned out she was more than right.

I lost my virginity when I was nineteen. That was around

1950. I knew little about birth control then. I was truly, truly ignorant. Happily, the first time I slept with a man, he was older and knew what to do. He used condoms, and that's when I found out about them. But I was such a timid person I never would ask a man, did he have any protection. I was a mere female, and females didn't ask men to make any kind of what I considered to be sacrifices; I was not to inconvenience them. That was my cultural upbringing.

The Pill wasn't around. I did not know about diaphragms until later and, even if I had, I couldn't go to a doctor and ask him about it—because I couldn't, it's that simple, because of my upbringing, the kind of person I was. I don't think I could acknowledge that I was really having sexual intercourse.

But I was terribly, terribly frightened of getting pregnant. Every time I had sex with a man, which wasn't often, I would go through a month of sheer terror, true fear and trembling, sweaty palms, being able to think of nothing else, which only goes to show you how strong the sex drive is and how natural. Despite all of that terror—and I'm talking tooth-gnashing terror—I still now and then would give in, succumb, to those pleasurable moments. It's astounding. When you're that scared you usually stay away from the thing that scares you, but not with sexuality.

I knew about abortion then. I knew it was a back alley kind of thing, I had heard stories. But you know, more than anything else, what scared me about getting pregnant was the shame of being found out as being a bad girl, being a bad person. I realize that a lot of that bad girl business has pursued me throughout much of my life. That was a big part of my psychotherapy. I went to therapy when I was about twenty-one, maybe even younger, and I had to deal with that in the most profound and tenacious way. To this day, I have to watch it and remind myself that I'm really a good person. It all goes back to the whole sexual, Catholic guilt business. I left it, but obviously *it* stayed with me.

I got pregnant when I was twenty-three, living in California, and a starlet. My breasts immediately became swollen and tender, and I just knew. I didn't take the test until I was almost sure, because I was frightened to death. When that period didn't come, I took the test, and sure enough, I was pregnant.

The man involved had been through this eighty thousand times with eighty thousand other women. He knew I wasn't ready for a child, and he wasn't about to take care of that responsibility. He also felt it was my fault for getting pregnant. No, he didn't use condoms, of course not. He wouldn't use anything; big men don't do things like that. By then, and at his insistence, I was using a diaphragm.

Once in a while, you didn't use the diaphragm when you felt it was fairly safe, but it's entirely possible I talked myself into thinking it was a safe time when in fact it was a dicey time. It was entirely possible that, being obsessed and mad about him, really nuts over him, I unconsciously thought, if I got pregnant, he would love me enough to marry me. It was one of those sad affairs where the love was unrequited in a way, so I will always suspect my motives at that time.

There was no chance that my lover was going to marry me. If he had said, "Let's get married," I very likely would have had that child, which would have been a horrendous mistake. It would have been simply a way to trap the man; God help the child who has to be born under those circumstances. If he had said, "I'll marry you," I would have told myself, "Oh, it's all going to be wonderful," because I was such a romantic girl in those days. That experience sort of wiped the romance out of my life forever.

If he wasn't going to marry me, I knew I was not prepared to bring up a child myself. And I didn't want to bring a child into the world and then give it away to somebody. To let people know I was pregnant, I felt, would have ruined my life. You mustn't forget that I was in the movies. I remember the people who were pregnant out of wedlock—now and then you heard. Remember Ingrid Bergman? She was the beacon that said to all other actresses: "You see what can happen if people find out." She was ostracized. She went to live in Italy. She didn't do films for *years.* And this was a great big luminary. So if that happened to her, what would happen to me and the rest of us who got pregnant?

If I had had to go to some strange land and get an abortion, that's probably what I would have done. The shame of it was so profound . . . it was a kind of terrorism that was practiced upon young women. That I was Puerto Rican made it even worse because Puerto Ricans were considered to be oversexed, dirty people. That hasn't changed a whole lot.

So it was immediately decided by both of us that I had to have an abortion. My lover found out about a doctor in Beverly Hills. What was very comforting about it was that the doctor was known for giving you an anesthetic, unlike a lot of the back alley experiences you heard about. But that was also very dangerous. You could die from a reaction to an anesthetic—it's happened in the dentist's chair. The danger was that it would be administered without the proper accouterments or assistance.

My lover didn't want to go with me. I think my friend dropped me off there and then came back for me. Interestingly enough, I was mostly afraid of being found out, that there would be a raid and it would come out that I was found in an abortion mill, unconscious.

I went to a real doctor's office. It was in the daytime. A woman admitted me. This doctor apparently did abortions when there was no one around. It was just too coincidental that the office was empty when I came in and empty when I left.

He took me into the room. He was a tall, slender, sleazy-looking, older man with no-color hair and a very dissipated face. It was never acknowledged that he was going to perform a curettage on me, so that made it all very scary. I guess if he had been up front and said, "Look, here's what we do . . . here's what happens when you wake up . . . here's what you do at home," it would have been okay. But he didn't behave like a doctor; he behaved like a criminal.

He used sodium pentothal. When I finally woke up, I remember looking at the clock and it was about two hours later, which was a long time. I said to him, "I want to see what you removed." I have a feeling I did that because I couldn't believe an abortion could be that easy, particularly after the horror stories I had heard from my girlfriends. When I woke up, I felt fine, nothing hurt, there was no blood around me. As a person riddled with guilt anyway, I thought, I don't deserve not to be in pain or suffering.

He got out a little tiny piece of gauze and showed me something about the size of the tip of my pinky fingernail, a little tiny piece of tissue. It was too small even for something in that earliest stage—I was less than two months pregnant. There was no blood, no nothing. I said, "That's it?" And he said, "Yep," and didn't want to talk anymore.

When it was over, I was really rather disoriented. I felt like a nonperson . . . like I had been stripped of an identity. I felt empty. I guess it was because my lover wanted me to have the abortion, because he didn't want our child, even though I didn't want it myself. It was an implicit rejection, a tacit expression of his feeling: Not with you. I wouldn't marry you. You're just not good enough for me. It only verified all the feelings I had about myself, that I didn't have much value as a person, that I was unworthy.

My friend took me home from the doctor's office, and I began to have cramps that night. She'd had an abortion—actually she'd had two, long ago, because she was older than I—and she said, "You shouldn't be feeling anything. You should feel fine." The next day I woke up in a pool of blood.

It didn't surprise me because I didn't know what to expect.

I told her that I was menstruating, and she said, "You shouldn't be doing that either." I wouldn't believe her. I kept saying, "Well, this man did a curettage and it makes sense that something's coming out." This went on for a whole week. The cramps got worse and worse; they were really severe, like labor pains. I kept bleeding. Finally, it got so bad that my friend said, "You have to see a doctor. Something is very wrong."

I went to my lover's doctor, reluctantly. He took one look and said, "You're going to the hospital . . . *now*." I said, "Will they arrest me? Will I go to jail?" That's how scared I was. He told me not to worry about that. He admitted me to Cedars Sinai Hospital in Los Angeles and finished the procedure. When I came out of the anesthesia, he told me I had had an incomplete abortion [tissue fragments are left inside]. He hadn't told me earlier because he didn't want to scare me, but he told me afterwards: "You could have died."

The reason I'm talking about this now is that I don't ever want that to happen to young girls again—it's a horror, a nightmare. Things have changed somewhat. Some of us have access to the Pill; some of us know enough about diaphragms and condoms. But a lot of us still don't and probably never will as long as Catholicism reigns supreme, as long as there's an image of a bad girl, and as long as sexuality is considered something dirty, particularly for girls.

Because of these things, there will always be unwanted pregnancies. Aside from the danger inherent for women when abortion is unavailable, there's the sad, sad reality of bringing up an unwanted child. That kills me almost more than anything else, when I see children who are being smacked around and abused because they weren't wanted in the first place.

But I feel very strongly that there's a cutoff point where it's just morally wrong to abort that baby—at six months, for sure. If these scientists tell me that baby can live outside the womb,

I'd have to say, "What took you so long to do it?" When a woman makes that decision that late, it does become murder to me. Then again, someone on the other side can say, "Yeah, but that was an ignorant girl; she didn't know any better." It's a very, very difficult question, but I'm absolute in my feeling about that cutoff point, except to save the mother's health or life, or in cases of rape or incest—although even then one can intercede soon after the event.

I never before talked about my abortion publicly. In fact, my daughter didn't know I had one. It's just that it never came up. When I told her I was going to do this book, she said, "My God, you never told me." She was absolutely shocked.

We have talked to her about sex, though. I remember when she was seventeen years old, we went into a long discussion with her one night at dinner. It wasn't about sex so much, but about getting pregnant. I talked *real* plain. I said, "I just have a feeling that you're getting ready. Without asking you whether you are or not, we need to know if you need to see a doctor, because what you don't want to do is get pregnant. You're not ready to have a baby, and you don't want to go through the horror of an abortion. Even though it's legal and safe, it's something you don't want to have to go through unless you must."

I didn't bring up my own abortion. I didn't want her to associate her own sexuality with my experience, which was really nightmarish. And AIDS didn't come up either; this was before AIDS.

We said all the things you should say about hormones and this overpowering desire and that sex is a very human thing. When our talk ended, we kissed her and hugged her. It was very moving, very touching. I got all teary-eyed. I am now. You see,

I wasn't just telling my daughter she wasn't bad for being sexual
. . . I was also telling *me*.

We never asked her anything after that. She went to the
doctor. Whether she did something that week or three months
later or that year, it was none of our business. She was safe. That
was the important thing.

J i l l   C l a y b u r g h

In the seventies and eighties, Jill Clayburgh brought to the big screen everyday women's triumphs over the turmoil in their postfeminist lives— at home, at work, and in bed. After struggling herself for nearly a decade for professional recognition, Clayburgh made her first mark on America's consciousness with her Emmy-nominated starring role in the television movie *Hustling.* She won the best actress award at the Cannes Film Festival for *An Unmarried Woman*, Oscar nominations for both *An Unmarried Woman* and *Starting Over*, and critical acclaim for her roles in *I'm Dancing As Fast As I Can* and *It's My Turn.*

Born in 1944, Clayburgh lives with husband/playwright David Rabe and an eight-year-old daughter, five-year-old son, and eighteen-year-old stepson in their home in upstate New York.

Birth control wasn't in the forefront of things you talked about in my house because there was certainly no expectation that a person of my age—fourteen, fifteen—was going to have sex. I think it came as a real shock to my parents that I had any kind of sexual experience. They found out because I got pregnant twice—in eighth grade, and again in ninth. It happened in the late fifties.

I would say that my early sexual experiences were very much a reaction to, a rebellion against my family. I had a troubled childhood. It wasn't that my family had serious problems of alcohol or abuse or were divorced or anything like that. I think my parents did their best, but I just didn't feel connected. I had a half brother, ten years older, and he never lived at home, and I had another brother, five years younger, who I wasn't very close to. I felt lost.

I also had very little sense of my own future. My eight-year-old daughter's always saying to me, "Well, I think I'll do this, and I'll be that. Could I be this *and* that? Could I be a piano player and a singer?" She's always thinking about the future. She says to me, "What did you want to be when you were a little girl?" and, really, I remember I had no image of adulthood for myself.

My having sex was a secret. I didn't have any girlfriends who were having sex. I was very, very isolated in this. I now have pretty close friends who I went to school with then. I think they knew, but it was something that they were very uncomfortable with. I sort of hung around with a group that wasn't at my school—a faster group, slightly older.

The boy was older, too. It was the same boy both times, and I was madly in love with him. I wasn't promiscuous.

I didn't know how to say no, and I didn't have enough self-esteem to understand the consequences of what I was doing. Besides, the notion of pregnancy was very foreign to me. If you'd asked me the facts of life, I think I could have told you, but I guess I thought: It's not going to happen to me.

I don't actually remember, on the first occasion that I got pregnant, penetration; my memory is fuzzy. I remember fooling around. Discovering that I was pregnant must have meant that I was pretty aware of my periods, which is amazing considering how unaware I was of everything else. I know I didn't want to have a baby.

Before I had the first abortion, my boyfriend got me the name of a gynecologist to see. I'll never forget it. Somehow, the gynecologist got the information to my boyfriend that clearly he could tell from the examination—from the shape of my vagina or some insanity—that I had slept with many, many people. I remember just being so stunned by that and hurt.

I don't think I was very pregnant either time—I must have been eight weeks. I remember the first time taking pills that were supposed to abort, called ergot [which cause uterine contractions], but they didn't work. I didn't get sick, but I think those pills can actually hurt you. I think I got them through that doctor.

The worst thing about getting pregnant was not knowing what to do and being scared that my parents would find out. I wanted to keep the pregnancy from them, but I had the sense not to let a friend steer me to some abortionist. I didn't have any money, for one thing; probably if I had the money I would have done it.

I went to my mother because I had nowhere else to go. I knew my mother well enough to know that the last thing she wanted was for her fourteen-year-old daughter to have a baby. My mother had gone to Radcliffe. I mean, there was no way I was going to be a fourteen-year-old teenage unwed mother. This was just not in the cards. I'm sure that she would have felt that this was the end of my life . . . I knew my mother was going to help me.

We never talked about adoption. I think adoption for me would have been so traumatic. To go through pregnancy, the hormonal changes, the growth of a child within you, leaving school, the social stigma—which at that time was very, very difficult—and childbirth, and then suddenly to have that baby taken away would have been the most cruel form of punishment. I really don't see how a child—and I consider myself at that time a child—could incorporate that into their understanding of life.

My mother told my father that I was pregnant. They kept it very much to themselves. Sometimes their anger about it came out in strange ways, where they would get angry about something that was not related to the abortion. But I really feel that they stuck with me in a big way.

I had the first abortion in a hospital in New York. I have very little recollection of it. I wasn't awake during the procedure. I think I was so out of touch with myself, I'm not even sure I felt fear. At fourteen, the last thing you're thinking about is, Will I be butchered? Will I be able to have children when I'm twenty-five? Someone who is so cut off from what's really going on as to get pregnant twice isn't thinking about consequences. You're just saying, "Let's get this over with . . ." Numb—numb was definitely the operative feeling.

I didn't walk out of that first abortion with any resolve to change what I was doing. I wanted to get back to my boyfriend. My parents tried to keep me from seeing him, but it didn't work. I remember my mother calling him a stinker and a bastard, and saying she wished she had a gun, she would shoot him in the eyes. But when you're in that sort of teenage love obsession, it's a very myopic point of view.

A very interesting thing happened between my mother and me after the first abortion. She very reluctantly said, "Well I guess you should have a diaphragm, and I'll help you get one." Then she backed down from it because she didn't want me to have sex. In those days fourteen was very—even in these days— it's very young.

That was just an indication of her ambivalence and how caught she was, and now I can completely identify with her. On the one hand, she wanted to protect me; on the other hand, she felt that would be a kind of encouragement, so she was torn. I absolutely wish she had given me birth control. Not giving someone birth control is not going to stop them from having sex; to make that decision, they have to come to a deeper understanding of whether or not sex is appropriate for them. To withhold birth control is only going to get them pregnant.

Actually, the second time I got pregnant, I think my boyfriend used a condom, but who knows if anybody knew then how to use them properly. When I went to my mother that time, I think she cried. My parents didn't know *what* to say. I scared them, and they must have felt pretty guilty too, thinking: Why is this human being behaving in this self-destructive fashion? Why is our daughter doing this? I don't know what they could have done at the time that would have been better; I'm just very, very fortunate that they were supportive. Mostly, I'm sorry that the only way I could express my own anger, my own dissatisfactions, was through such self-abuse.

I went with my mother to Puerto Rico for the second abortion. There were all these people in the waiting room, and I woke up in a ward. It was a hospital that seemed as if it had been bombed; it was not quite all built or it was falling apart. Of course, parts of the experience are just dream images by this point. . . .

I remember the doctor being very sweet. Some of these doctors were saints; I think the one in Puerto Rico was. One of the things you deal with when you're fourteen is incredible guilt . . . anybody can just get to your guilt. But in the case of both people who gave me the abortions, I remember sympathy and kindness. I really did not feel that I was getting punished by them. I was punishing myself and punishing other people enough.

The abortions were harrowing in the context of my life, in the way they made me feel, so isolated, like a freak—other girls were playing volleyball. The actual abortions were not harrowing. I would credit that to the fact that my parents researched the situation as well as they could and had the money to get me safe and decent abortions. It's more in retrospect that I appreciate how lucky I was. I was completely lucky.

As for the children I would have had, the worst punishment for any offspring would have been to be the child of me. At that age, I was very unbalanced. If I had had a baby, I would have been the worst mother in the world, and I would have raised a very, very disturbed child because I was obviously barely ready to deal with my own self, my own feelings, who I was. It would have been the end of my life and the end of this child's life.

There is an attitude that teenagers are wildly irresponsible and that making abortions illegal will affect their level of responsibility, which it won't. I mean, I'm a case in point. Abortion wasn't legal, but I was completely not careful. And they're saying that most teenagers don't use condoms. So what is that telling you? Teenagers don't use their brains! They're not thinking. But I don't believe they should be punished for the rest of their lives because they have this mental derangement for a few years.

Therapy is what pulled me out of that self-destructive pattern . . . therapy and wanting to act. When I got a direction for my life, it changed radically. Once I had a direction, I was as driven about acting as I had been about my boyfriend.

Getting back to the abortions, do you want to know if I thought of the fetus as a living being? At that time, it never crossed my mind. What I really feel today—and this is not a popular pro-choice point of view—is that a fetus is alive from the moment of conception. I don't think that we should say it isn't alive until such and such a week or month . . . it's always alive. Women know the first week they're pregnant. That's where we get into trouble, because it's a very mushy argument— six weeks, eight weeks, ten weeks. Bullshit! You're not a little bit alive, and you're not a little bit dead.

It's alive, but that still doesn't make it your responsibility to sacrifice both your life and this child's life. The position is not about whether or not it's alive; it's about whether or not someone wants to give birth and have the responsibility of another human being with them for the rest of their life. It's about being a parent, about being a mother, about being a father, about being a decent parent, about the most important, difficult thing that you're going to do in your life. It takes incredible energy and love to be a good parent and sometimes it's not the right time.

I think once you get to a certain age, once you've had children, the idea of an abortion is very, very painful. I almost had another abortion at forty-four, and I would say I was *keenly* aware that this was a potential life. Prior to that, I'd had a miscarriage in the fifth month. Then . . . I had a baby. Then, I had another baby. And then, I had a pregnancy where I was up against it so hard in terms of trying to decide whether or not I wanted to have this baby.

It was three years ago this spring. I'd been very sick with the flu for ten days, had a 104-degree fever, and lost track of when I was fertile, so I didn't use birth control when I should have. I got pregnant, and I was in a total state of conflict.

One day I could handle it and felt that—even though my second pregnancy had been very difficult and very exhausting—I could get through it. I'd wake up and say, "I have such a beautiful family, and this has just happened, and how am I to say what is best? Clearly you can't control your destiny. I'll have this baby, and it'll be another wonderful human being . . . the most incredible person, just like my other children. There's no way I'm going to get an abortion." The next day I just felt, "I can't do it . . . I can't have a third infant who is going to be seven when I'm fifty . . . I don't have the strength for it. It's unfair to my family, it's going to take so much out of me, it's going to take so much of me away from them. I have to have an abortion." I went back and forth, and back and forth. It was horrible.

I called my gynecologist and said, "Make an appointment for an abortion." I had the appointment scheduled for nine-fifteen on a Wednesday morning. The night before, my husband and I made a date to go for a drive and talk about it. I remember all the little green buds were coming out where I live. My husband was very, very thoughtful. We talked about who would make the money, which year, if I had the child. He said, "I will cover the finances for the next three years . . . you don't have to work." He also said, "If you're really this much up in the air about it, I would much rather that you did not have an abortion. But if you want one, go right ahead."

I could not make the choice to have an abortion because I didn't need one . . . I didn't need one. We're talking about a person with a certain amount of money, a family, a husband. It didn't seem right to me. In a way, I was jubilant about it then—I really wanted to have this baby—but I still went back and forth. It was unbelievable. And I was having so much trouble with the pregnancy, it was such a hard pregnancy.

Several months later, at the end of the third month, I had a miscarriage. Frankly, I think the miscarriage was related to this new test that they're giving earlier than amniocentesis—CVS [chorionic villus sampling]. Since I took it, it has come more under question; at that time, the statistics were off about how dangerous it was. I had the test, and ten days later I had the miscarriage. Again, I felt very conflicted. I just don't know. Thank God I didn't have to make the choice.

Nora Sayre

Nora Sayre made her reputation as a writer who analyzed a frequently chaotic American cultural and political scene. A former film critic for *The New York Times*, she is the author of *Sixties Going on Seventies*, which was nominated for a National Book Award, and *Running Time: Films of the Cold War*.

Daughter of writer Joel Sayre, she grew up mainly in New York City. Sayre is divorced, and still lives in Manhattan. Her forthcoming book is about the 1950s; she describes it as "cultural history: a memoir of mentalities."

I was a student at Radcliffe at the time of my abortion. It was summer vacation, not in the middle of exam period, at least. I had a summer job here in New York, which was fortunate, because trying to find an abortion in Boston in the fifties would have been a nightmare. Boston was an *ultra* Catholic town.

I was living with a young man, but there was another young woman sharing the apartment for cover. A lot of people think of the fifties as a time when nobody went to bed together under a certain age, but plenty did. And quite a few of us got pregnant while using vaginal foam, a common form of birth control in that era.

When I found I was pregnant, there was no question whatsoever in my mind or the young man's that an abortion was necessary. It was inconceivable that I would be able to go back to college pregnant; I'm sure that any college would have expelled a pregnant unmarried undergraduate at that time, although I think some graduate schools were more tolerant. The young man and I had a horrified view of shotgun marriages; we didn't even consider marriage.

I did not go to my parents for two reasons. They were very much of the 1920s generation, and I knew they had had lots of affairs before marriage, and certainly some afterward. But we just didn't confide much in parents in those days, even if we got on well with them; that's very true of my generation.

Moreover, my mother had had a very severe nervous breakdown. When somebody's in bad shape, you're afraid of triggering all sorts of things. My father was struggling with the consequences of my mother's illness, and my abortion would have been upsetting for both of them. Besides, parents are not often as rational about their own daughter's pregnancy as they might be about someone else's. And you don't want to burden yourself with your parents' being upset.

Fortunately, we knew quite a few seasoned, older people in their thirties. We had a friend who knew just the right doctor and arranged the abortion for me. It was very reassuring to know that the friend had had an abortion with the same doctor.

The doctor was a distinguished gynecologist, and I really want to pay some tributes to her. She was sixty-something, a feminist, and a refugee from Vienna who probably had come to the United States in the thirties. She was both stern and sympathetic—stern because discretion was essential. She kept stressing that doctors could go to jail for abortions; they were watched. some of them, by the police. She told us, "You must never mention your abortion in a taxicab because some taxi drivers blackmail doctors." So one's sense of the illegality was powerful.

This doctor would perform only a small number of abortions per year; she did them because she was a feminist. She had a great sympathy for students; she thought it was simply terrible for anyone's education to be interrupted. She also thought shotgun marriages were dreadful, and that young women should proceed with their lives as they normally would. She insisted on seeing the man too, if possible, because she didn't think an unwanted pregnancy was just the woman's problem. We were charged three hundred dollars. She was hardly doing it to get rich; I had heard that most abortions cost eight hundred dollars.

The young man I was involved with took me to the doctor's office in Manhattan, in a hotel that no longer exists. One thing I remember—this is a powerful memory—is that the office was being used at night. It had to be about eight o'clock. The doctor would never have done it during her regular office hours when the nurse was around. She didn't trust the nurse. This doctor knew the whole world of blackmail, arrest, and jail.

Once I was inside the room, the doctor and the anesthetist— who I did not know at the time was her husband—put tape all around the edges of the doors so that no light would show through, so no one would see that the offices were being used.

I came out of the anesthesia saying, "You didn't give me enough. I'm awake." Those kindly voices said in Viennese accents, "But it's over . . . it's all over." Then one was offered tea and cookies, which the husband, the anesthetist, had baked. But they wanted you to leave as soon as you were able to. You didn't have to go rushing out that minute—there was time for cookies and a little wind-down conversation—but they gave you a shot to wake you up so you wouldn't be lying there for hours.

I found, when I saw the mirror on the wall, that the doctor had put round circles of rouge on my face—these rather European, Viennese, bright red circles—so that the postabortion pallor wouldn't be noticed by the doorman downstairs. Now this was a big building; people would be coming up and down in the elevators to and from their rooms. She said, "When you're walking out, if you suddenly feel a little weak, take your boyfriend's arm, but also pretend you're drunk so nobody will be able to guess."

After the abortion, the overpowering feeling was one of such relief: You thought, It's over, and you're still here. But the next day, you can get depressed as hell. I think the hormonal turnaround is a great part of it. And at an early age—it might be different for someone older—it's your first brush with what could have been death, which you probably had never really thought about. Abortion was something other people died of; you hadn't. There was some sense of having looked into the abyss.

I will add that I never felt the fetus was a person. I didn't then; I don't now. But naturally, you do think of the person who might have been. You could briefly cheer yourself up by thinking of the worst characteristics in both your families, but still, you do have the sense of the loss of a potential person.

Returning to college after my abortion, I found myself—not that I would have foreseen or planned this—arranging New York abortions for students in Cambridge, Massachusetts. When a best friend's friend got caught—once again, the vaginal foam—I said that I would try to arrange something, but I couldn't promise. I had to be certain about the discretion of those concerned. I really felt protective of this doctor; I believed every word she said—and still do—about the dangers for her.

I must have arranged five, I would say. The form would be, we'd go together to New York. I would have an appointment to see the doctor as though for a checkup—because again, you mustn't give anything away in front of the nurse. I would be having the routine examination, and I would say, "Another friend of mine, majoring in Medieval history"—the doctor liked to know majors because she took education very, very seriously—"needs help." I had to plead the case, and I was always in great suspense as to whether she would do it.

She did it each time because it was another student. One of them was the only person I knew who did try to find an abortion in Boston. She had a horrible experience. The doctor she went to was examining her to see if she was pregnant, and he started fooling around. When I told my doctor about that, she became so angry that she said, "Of course I'll do it."

Some years later, a friend of mine, who was married with two children and very little money, felt she must have an abortion. My doctor was not available. Mutual friends found someone in New Jersey, and my friend went to him. Afterwards, she said it was arranged through his answering service, and the waiting room was full of women who were there to get abortions. A couple of months later, I picked up the *Post* and saw that this doctor had been busted; he went to jail with quite a long sentence. My doctor was right; her doctor was wrong. He hadn't been discreet.

When abortion became legal in New York State in 1970, my immediate thought was for a bunch of us to take my doctor to dinner. I called a friend and found out the doctor had died a year or two before. I was very sad to hear that. I can't imagine what some of us would have done without her.

For years, you did have to keep your abortion a secret. There are some kinds of secrets that people rather enjoy having; they know something others don't know, and it makes them feel a bit superior. But this secrecy was a burden.

Many of us who had abortions did a fine job of fooling everybody. We had abortions right under the noses of our parents; we spared them. And we told few of our friends. A couple of weeks after my abortion, I was spending a weekend in the country with a very good friend to whom I would have told almost anything. But I was so schooled by my doctor about the need for secrecy that I didn't tell her. My friend later said that I had been miles away that weekend—very distant—and she thought that for some reason she couldn't fathom we were no longer friends.

Eventually I told my father, which I had not planned to do. I had terrible times with menstrual periods through the years and went to several doctors for different treatments, pills, and shots. Nothing worked. I never talked any gynecology with my father, but he realized that my periods all too often made me absolutely useless. He urged me to go to a doctor who was a friend of his, a GP he had known during World War II. I'd met this guy a couple of times—he was a very pleasant, affable man —but I was quite sure that if I told him about my abortion, he would tell my father.

Finally my father and I had a lively argument. He began insisting I go to this doctor, and I refused. This was making no sense, so I told him about the abortion. He was immensely sympathetic, which was no great surprise. His first question was, "Was the man you were involved with nice?" I said, "Yes, indeed he was." Then he wanted to know who it was. I said, "That's our business," and he said, "You're right." Then I learned some more family history. He said he knew it was hell for a woman, then added, "Think of the poor guy standing outside waiting." I found out that both he and my mother had been through abortions.

I never thought of telling my great-aunt, a suffragist who lived to the age of ninety-four. She had a somewhat Victorian viewpoint and would have been very disturbed at the idea of sex outside of marriage. To a lot of feminists of that era, that generation, who lived and died virgins, sex was something that men did to women. It was a mystery, a misery, but women went through it in order to have what she called "a nice baby." Then around 1970—when she was ninety—after she'd listened to a radio call-in show about abortion, she surprised me by saying: "I think an abortion would be sheer poetry compared to an unwanted child."

Ursula K. Le Guin

Ursula K. Le Guin is a novelist, poet, short-story writer, critic, and essayist. She established her reputation in science fiction with the Hainish novels, which include *The Left Hand of Darkness* and *The Dispossessed,* and in fantasy with the first three of the Earthsea books: *A Wizard of Earthsea, The Tombs of Atuan,* and *The Farthest Shore.* Her most recent books are 1990's *Tehanu,* last of the Earthsea series; *Searoad,* stories of the Oregon coast; and two picture books, *A Ride on the Red Mare's Back* and *Fish Soup.* She has received many awards, including five Hugos, four Nebulas, a Pushcart Prize, a Newbery Honor Medal, a National Book Award, and the Harold D. Vursell Award from the American Academy and Institute of Arts and Letters. The following piece, originally titled "The Princess," first appeared in her collection of essays *Dancing at the Edge of the World,* published by Grove Press in 1989, and then in the January/February 1989 issue of *Ms.* magazine under the title "So Much for Prince Charming."

Le Guin was born in 1929 to anthropologist Alfred Louis Kroeber and writer Theodora Kroeber. She grew up in California, attended Radcliffe, graduating in 1951, and two years later married historian Charles Le Guin, with whom she lives in Portland, Oregon. She has two daughters, one son, and one granddaughter.

Once upon a time, long, long ago, in the Dark Ages, there was a princess. She was wealthy, well fed, well educated, and well beloved. She went to a college for training female royalty, and there, at the associated college for training male royalty, she met a prince. He, too, was wealthy, well fed, well educated, and well beloved. And they fell in love with each other and had a really royal time.

Although the princess was on the Honors List and the prince was a graduate student, they were remarkably ignorant about some things. The princess's parents, though modest and even inhibited, had been responsible and informative: she knew all about how babies are made. She had read books about it. But it had not occurred to her parents or the people who wrote the books that she might need to know how to *keep from making babies.* This was long ago, remember, in the Dark Ages, before sex was obligatory, before the Pill. All she knew was there was something called a rubber, and boys always sniggered when the Trojan War was mentioned in high school. The prince, of course, knew everything. He'd been around. He'd had sex since he was fifteen, he said. He knew you had to wear a condom the first time each night. But the second or third time each night, you didn't. It was safe. He knew that.

Perhaps you can imagine what happens next in this story? Like all fairy tales, it follows a familiar path; there is a certain inevitable quality to the events.

"We have to get married!" the princess said to the prince.

"I'm going home to my mother," the prince said to the princess.

And he did. He went home to his family palace in Brooklyn Heights, and hid in the throne room.

The princess went to her family palace on Riverside Drive and cried a lot. She cried the Hudson River full of tears. But, though she had never been punished for anything in her life, she could not bring herself to tell her parents why she was crying. She made up a pretext to go to her mother's gynecologist and get a pregnancy test. They used rabbits; if the test was positive, the rabbit died; remember, this is the Dark Ages. The rabbit died. The princess didn't tell her parents, but went and dug the prince out and said, "We *really* have to get married."

"You're not a member of my religion, and anyhow, it's your baby," said the prince, and went back to Brooklyn Heights. And she went back home and cried so hard that her parents finally saw what had to be the matter. And they said, "Okay, it's okay, honey, and if he won't marry you, you don't have to have the baby."

Now, you may recall that in the Dark Ages abortion was not legal. It was a crime, and not a minor one.

The princess's parents were not criminal types. They were the kind of people who obey the speed limit, and pay taxes and parking-ticket fines, and return borrowed books. I mean they were honest. They were neither square nor unsophisticated, they were not "religious," but they were intensely moral people, with a love of kindness and decency, and a strong respect for the law. And yet now, without hesitation, they resolved to break the law, to conspire to commit a felony. And they did so in the reasoned and deeply felt conviction that it was right, that indeed it was their *responsibility*, to do so.

The princess herself questioned the decision, not on legal grounds, of course, but ethically. She cried some more and said, "I'm being cowardly. I'm being dishonest. I'm evading the consequence of my own action."

Her father said, "That's right. You are. The cowardice, dishonesty, evasion, is a lesser sin than the crass irresponsibility of sacrificing your training, your talent, and the children you will want to have, in order to have one nobody wants to have."

He was a Victorian, you see, and a bit of a Puritan. He hated waste and wastefulness.

So the princess and her parents tried to find out how to get an abortion—and they got a little panicky, because they didn't know anybody who knew. The gynecologist got huffy when asked for a reference. "I don't handle A.B.s," he said. After all, his license to a lucrative practice was at stake; he could have gone to jail; you can't blame him. It was an old family friend, a child psychologist, who finally found the right contact, the criminal connection. She made an appointment for "an examination."

They were really slick, that outfit. Dr. So-and-So. Nice office on the Lower East Side, polite smiling receptionist, *Esquire* and *National Geographic* on the waiting room tables. Their reputation was "the highest-class abortionists in New York City," and it was probably deserved. They charged more for an abortion than most working families made in a year. This was no dirty backroom business. It was clean. It was class. They never said the word "abortion," not even that cute euphemism "A.B." The doctor offered to restore the hymen. "It's easy," he said. "No extra charge." The princess did not wish to be rebuilt like a Buick and said, "No. Get on with it." And they did. Did a fine job, I'm sure. As the princess left that office she passed a girl coming in, a college girl with red eyes and fear in her face, and she wanted to stop and say, "It's okay, it's not so bad, don't be afraid," but she was afraid to. And she went back uptown in a taxi with her mother, both of them crying, partly out of grief, partly out of relief. "The endless sorrow . . ."

The princess went back to college to finish her degree. From time to time she would see the prince lurking and scuttling around behind the ivy on the buildings. I'm sure he has lived happily ever after. As for the princess, she got her B.A. a few months after she got her A.B., and then went on to graduate school, and then got married, and was a writer, and got pregnant by choice four times. One pregnancy ended in spontaneous abortion, miscarriage, in the third month; three pregnancies ended in live normal birth. She had three desired and beloved children, none of whom would have been born if her first pregnancy had gone to term.

If any birth is better than no birth, and more births are better than fewer births, as the "Right-to-Life" people insist, then they should approve of my abortion, which resulted in three babies instead of one. A curious but logical method of achieving their goal! But the preservation of life seems to be rather a slogan than a genuine goal of the anti-abortion forces; what they want is control. Control over behavior: power over women. Women in the anti-choice movement want to share in male power over women, and do so by denying their own womanhood, their own rights and responsibilities.

If there is a moral to my tale, it's something like this. In spite of everything the little princess had been taught by the male-supremacist elements of her society, by high school scandals about why Sallie dropped out of school in March, by novels extolling motherhood as woman's sole function, by the gynecologist's furtiveness, by the existence of a law declaring abortion to be a crime, by the sleek extortionism of the abortionist—despite all those messages repeating ABORTION IS WRONG!—when terror was past, she pondered it all, and she thought, "I have done the right thing."

What was wrong was not knowing how to prevent getting pregnant. What was wrong was my ignorance. To legislate that ignorance, that's the crime. I'm ashamed, she thought, for letting bigots keep me ignorant, and for acting willfully in my ignorance, and for falling in love with a weak, selfish man. I am deeply ashamed. But I'm not guilty. Where does guilt come in? I did what I had to do so that I could do the work I was put here to do. I will do that work. That's what it's all about. It's about taking responsibility.

So I thought at the time, not very clearly. That I can think more clearly about it now, and talk, and write about it, is entirely due to the moral courage and strength of women and men who have been working these thirty years for the rights and dignity and freedom of women, including the right to abortion. They set me free.

Why did I tell you this tale, which is only too familiar? Well, I called myself a princess in it, partly for the joke, and partly because my parents were indeed royal, where it counts, in the soul; but also to keep reminding myself that *I was privileged.* I had "the best abortion in New York City." What was it like, in the Dark Ages when abortion was a crime, for the girl whose dad couldn't borrow the cash, as my dad could? What was it like for the girl who couldn't even tell her dad, because he'd go crazy with shame and rage? Who couldn't tell her *mother*? Who had to go alone to that filthy room and put herself body and soul into the hands of a professional criminal?—because that's what every doctor who did an abortion was, whether he was an extortionist or an idealist.

I told this fable to a group of people a few years ago. What is frightening to me is that it has become out of date, only in no longer being urgent enough. The threat to freedom of choice is greater now than at any time since *Roe* v. *Wade*. The need for action and solidarity is immediate. We are not going back to the Dark Ages. We are not going to let anybody in this country have that kind of power over any girl or woman. There are great powers, outside the government and in it, trying to legislate the return of darkness. We are not great powers. But we are the light. Nobody can put us out. May we shine very bright and steady, today and always.

B a r b a r a   C o r d a y

Barbara Corday co-created the groundbreaking, Emmy Award—winning, female buddy television series *Cagney and Lacey.* She has been director and vice president of comedy series development at ABC; president of Columbia Pictures Television; and executive vice president of Primetime Programs for CBS Entertainment, which made her the highest ranking woman in network television.

Once divorced and once separated, Corday, forty-seven, has a daughter from her first marriage; three stepdaughters from her second marriage; and one stepgranddaughter. She lives in Los Angeles, where she is a frequent spokeswoman for the Voters for Choice, a political action committee, and the California Abortion Rights Action League.

At the time of my abortion, I was going out with a man who was much older than I and a very successful executive. Luckily, really, he wasn't a kid like I was. He was able to give me some money. My memory is that he gave me five hundred dollars for the actual abortion, and I paid my plane fare from New York to Miami.

There was a lot of fear and trepidation about having the abortion. I was afraid that I was doing something that was horribly underground, underworld, underbelly of society. The fear of the man who performed the abortion, and the people around him, was that I would lead The Law to them. That was a very big part of the trauma of the day.

I went to Miami alone. When I got off the plane, I rented a car and drove to the address I had been given, which in fact was not the address where the doctor was, nor was it the address where the operation was going to be performed. They made me wait there for hours to see if I had been followed. Then, they left my rented car at this address, put me in another car with two men who were Cuban and didn't speak English, and took me to another address. I had no idea where I was, where I was going, who I was with.

The circuitous route you had to take to get to the person who was actually going to do this thing for you made you feel very much like what I imagine a drug user feels today trying to score. It seemed to me that it involved the same type of secrecy and fear—making phone calls to numbers where somebody has to call you back, leaving a message, writing to a post office box, skulking around. You felt very dirty. You felt like a criminal. It was incredibly humiliating.

I was very scared, and I think the only thing that kept me going was knowing what it would mean if I turned around and left. Where was I going to get better care? What was going to be different about the next place that I would go to? And the clock was ticking; you're only in your first couple of months for so long.

This was 1962 or 1963, and I was eighteen or nineteen years old. I'd started working right out of high school and was a very young, beginning publicist. I had grown up always wanting to be older, and I was only sixteen when I moved to New York City and into my own apartment. My roommate, a Rockette, and I shared a studio—one huge room with a little kitchen on the Upper West Side.

Although I was raised in the fifties in Brooklyn, somehow I was not raised in that traditional Jewish, you're-going-to-get-married-and-have-babies kind of way. My mother had had a long career as an entertainer—a singer and a comedian—and my mother's mother and sister were both entertainers. My focus growing up, especially after we moved to Florida, was to get back to New York and get to work. My parents were fine about my going out on my own. All of the kids in my mother's family were on the road and working when they were teenagers.

When I found out I was pregnant, I didn't go to my parents. By the time you were the age I was, going to your parents would have meant building on conversations about sex that had happened years ago, and those conversations hadn't happened in my family. And when you're older, you probably get more from your friends . . . your contemporaries.

I did not think then that my parents had access to help, and I do not think so now. Besides, I didn't go to my mother because I was sure she would have worried about me. If I had said to her, I'm going mountain climbing, she would have worried, so given the illegality of the situation, she would certainly have worried. I don't believe that my parents would have been disapproving; they were not disapproving people. They were always very much behind me; whatever I was doing was always seen as being a good thing.

Part of the reason I went for the abortion by myself was financial. Who was going to fly with me to Florida? The man just gave me the money and said, "Go take care of it," which was very common at the time. Men's consciousness was certainly no better than ours was, and ours was not so great. It seemed normal for me to do this on my own. I don't even remember being angry at him that he didn't come with me or participate.

The two young men who picked me up in Miami took me to a small apartment building, I would guess a mile or two away. We went into this apartment. There were people in the living room; I have no idea who they were. There were children. We went to the back of the apartment where there was a very large walk-in closet that was outfitted as an operating room, and they put me on a table. They had makeshift stirrups hanging from the ceiling, like ropes. I put my legs into them.

I had been told that the man who was going to do the abortion was a Cuban doctor who was not allowed to practice in the United States. It is certainly possible that he was; it is certainly possible that he wasn't. I don't have the slightest way of knowing. He was a tall, attractive, gray-haired man, and he was very nice to me. He told me what he was going to do. I was very scared and didn't really hear. He told me they were not able to give any anesthetic, which, of course, we know today is what most complications come from in surgery. If there had been a complication, there was nothing they could do.

The two guys who had brought me there stayed, and eventually I was very glad because they held my hands. They told me I couldn't scream because somebody would hear me. I cried a lot but I didn't scream. It was pretty excruciating, and my ankles were all rubbed from the ropes that my legs were hanging in. I guess I had a D&C—they did a scraping. The fact that I didn't go into shock was really amazing.

When the doctor was finished, he told me to go see my doctor as soon as I got to New York, just in case there was anything that needed to be done. I was bleeding, but I couldn't lie there for any amount of time. They took me back to my rental car. I sat in the car for about half an hour, then drove to the airport, got on a plane, and went back to New York.

The next day I saw my doctor in New York, and he said they had done a very decent job. He knew I'd been pregnant because he was the one who told me, but he'd also told me there was nothing he could do. That was the hardest part of all. He felt badly that there was nothing he could do, and I certainly never quite felt the same toward him after that.

I had an abortion because I believed that there wasn't any other alternative. The truth is that I never had a moment of thinking I was going to have a baby. It was not an option that I would have considered for five seconds. I was probably making a hundred dollars a week, and it would have been an impossible situation. I would have been a nineteen-year-old mother—a nineteen-year-old *single* mother. Anybody knows what that means.

And in 1962, it was far less shameful, if you will, to have an abortion than it was to have a baby. Having a baby out of wedlock would have been a very shocking thing then, whereas today, I have a hundred friends who have babies without having husbands.

It is very hard for us to cast our minds back to that time in terms of sexual mores, but it was really before the women's movement, before the sexual revolution, before Vietnam, before hippies. People didn't live together then. If you were sleeping with someone, you had sex, you got up, you got dressed, you got in a taxi, and you went home. Even if you went home at five o'clock in the morning when the light was coming up, you went home. You did not sleep over at a man's apartment, a man did not sleep over at your apartment, and you certainly did not move in with someone.

Actually, the sexual revolution had a little bit begun in the sense that more young women were having premarital sex, but it was as if you weren't admitting it because you slept at home. Everybody knew that everybody was doing it, but you didn't talk about it.

I don't believe that I was using birth control at the time I got pregnant, nor had I used it up to then. I've never had a diaphragm in my life, which a lot of women did in those early days; I didn't like the idea of putting a foreign object inside of me.

I think that I was more careful after the abortion—less reckless, sexually, less inclined to have sex without fear or thought to the consequences. But I didn't start using birth control until the Pill was really considered safe, when I got married in 1966.

Why? I don't know. Partly because, once you got birth control, then you were saying, "I have affairs," and we weren't able to say that. The other answer is youth. The younger you are, the less you believe that anything bad can happen to you. It's riding a motorcycle without a helmet, it's driving after drinking, it's all the things you did that when you're forty, you look back on and say, "How could I have been so stupid?"

It took me a while to get over the trauma of my abortion—not of losing a baby, because I must say I have always believed and still do that at that moment it is not a baby. When I was twenty-three and pregnant with my daughter, I still believed that. I was happy in anticipating the birth of a child because I was married and ready to have a baby, but I didn't regard her as a child until she was there as a child.

As a mother now, I am convinced that if my daughter needed an abortion, I would be the person to know about it because she is the kind of kid who does tell me stuff. As a matter of fact, when my daughter was in high school, one of her girlfriends had an abortion, and it was my house that they came back to afterwards. Her friend felt that she couldn't tell her mother. I tried to encourage her to, but I did not pick up the phone and tell her mother myself.

I think laws forcing kids to notify their parents are horrible. It's hard, but we know too many stories about rape and incest and alcoholic parents and violent parents to be comfortable saying that a girl has to tell. I am absolutely willing to risk not knowing in order to protect the girls who would suffer in the telling.

I also have had a legal abortion in my life. I went to Cedars Sinai Hospital in Los Angeles, with my own gynecologist who had delivered my kid, and it was an entirely different situation. The emotion? Well, in a funny way I think I had much more emotion about doing that.

I was much older—thirty-two, I guess. I was newly in love.

My second husband and I were not yet married, but we were living together. My doctor had said if I ever wanted to have more children, it would be very difficult, so I was not very thoughtful about birth control in those years. I also felt, if it happens, it happens, because I'm in this relationship, and it will be okay. I think people feel that way a lot, but sometimes you discover it's not okay. The man absolutely did not want any more children. He already had three, I had one, and four kids seemed like plenty.

Although I agreed philosophically that we didn't need to have any more children, when I was pregnant I certainly would have gone either way. I don't think I was that hot to have an abortion, but he felt very strongly about it, and since we were not yet married, the strength of his feelings versus the ambivalence on my part won out. So I went to Cedars Sinai and had the abortion. I had my tubes tied at the same time so that I would not have to deal with that anymore.

I've never been sorry, really, that I didn't have that child; I've never had any second thoughts. But I did definitely have more of an emotional reaction to having that abortion all those years later because I was in love with the person that I was pregnant by, and we ultimately did get married . . . you know, we would have a thirteen-year-old kid today. I think it was a very different situation.

L i n d a   E l l e r b e e

For the past twenty years, Linda Ellerbee has earned a living in television, winning seven Emmys along the way. She has been a network correspondent at ABC and NBC, where she also anchored and wrote the award-winning newsmagazine *Weekend* and the pioneering late-night news program *NBC News Overnight.* In 1987, she left the networks to form her own company, Lucky Duck Productions, to produce programs for network syndication, cable, and public television. Lucky Duck is currently producing a newsmagazine series for kids on Nickelodeon.

On the print front, Ellerbee has written two best-selling books. Her first, *And So It Goes,* is about network television; it was nominated for a Pulitzer Prize. Her latest, *Move On,* is about surviving the last half of the twentieth century with one's sense of humor intact. She also writes a nationally syndicated newspaper column for the Hearst Company's King Features Syndicate.

Born in 1944, married four times and divorced, Ellerbee has two grown children. She lives with Rolfe Tessem, her partner in Lucky Duck Productions.

I went to a doctor I found in the yellow pages using an assumed name, an assumed married name, and took the test. I called back later to get the results and he said, "Oh, congratulations! Mrs. Jones, you're pregnant." I remember sort of sinking down into the chair at the other end, and being so caught up in the lie that I smiled and said, "Oh, yes. Thank you." Then I hung up the phone and sat there, small and shivering and frightened to death.

I did not know what to do. So I did what women did then: I asked around. Actually, I was too cowardly to ask. You see, every time a woman would say, "I have a friend who's in trouble," everyone would think it was *that* woman. So I asked my roommate who worked at a television network to ask there for an unnamed friend of hers. She then asked a braver friend of hers to be the one to do the asking.

We found someone who knew someone, and there were phone calls, and he agreed to come to my apartment in Chicago one night, Friday, at midnight. I was to have six hundred dollars cash. That was a lot of money in 1965. Volkswagens, new, cost less than a thousand dollars then! I didn't have six hundred dollars in cash—I was making sixty-five dollars a week.

My parents were in Houston, Texas, where I grew up, and the last thing in the world I wanted was for them to find out. I thought if I told my mother that life would come to an end! To me it was so out of the realm of anything I'd ever discussed with my parents that I couldn't even imagine such a thing. I figured that they would think I was horrible; they would feel disgraced; they would have no respect for me. Having disappointed them in my marriage—I'd married at nineteen and it lasted seven months—I wanted so desperately to prove to them that I was a grown-up. This would be the final thing to prove to them that I wasn't.

If abortion had been legal but required parental consent at the time, I probably would have been such a coward that I would have sought out an illegal abortion or something that didn't require parental consent. My civil liberties heart says no to those laws; if a woman is old enough to conceive, it's her business and her right.

But, knowing what I know now about my mother and me, the fact is that the best thing that could have happened would have been if I had told her. In the latter part of her life, when I was older, she and I got to know one another, and I found out I had spent a lot of years selling my mother short. She was not the old fuddy-duddy that I always assumed. I could have told this woman anything, and she was there for me in ways I never knew.

The man I was having an affair with in Chicago—that's really a grown-up word for what was going on—was just a couple of years older than I was, and I was nearly twenty-one, and probably his ignorance was as great as mine. He told me that certain times of day, of year, of month, of week, I wouldn't get pregnant and not to worry. I believed it.

I did not tell the man that I was pregnant. I was in love with him, but I did not wish to be married to him. I think I felt then that it was an entirely personal decision, totally my decision. I've come to change my mind about that. Today, I would say it is *primarily* the woman's decision but not entirely. It is as wrong to exclude men from this decision and this process as it is to say they should make the total decision. But I don't think they have a right to veto it.

So I went to my boss at the radio station where I worked, because nobody my age *had* six hundred dollars, no one I knew. He was a self-made man who founded a company called Chess Checker Cadet Records. He made a lot of money off Chuck Berry, Ramsey Lewis, a lot of black artists. I thought of him because he had had a hard life. He had been an immigrant, a German or Russian Jew, done well, built his company. I told him the truth because I couldn't think of a lie good enough. I thought that he would understand that bad things sometimes happen to good people, as we learned to say. Nothing could have been further from the truth.

He had me stand in his office, and he yelled at me. He yelled not just about what a slut I was, but on and on about how this proved why women shouldn't work because I should have been home having babies to begin with and not taking a job from some man—now, mind you, this man had hired me—and this was just what you'd expect from sluts who worked.

I felt *shamed*. I could feel myself starting to cry because, like many people and especially women when we get very angry, we cry. I have always had that problem. I don't think I have penis envy; I envy the power that has always gone with penises. I've always envied in men their ability to get truly angry and not cry. My eyes were burning, I could feel my face burning, and my anger was such that I wanted to stalk out of the room, I wanted to tell him what I thought of him, but I couldn't because I needed the money.

He finally agreed and charged me quite a lot of interest, far over the going rate of a bank loan. I made up a payment schedule so that he could deduct it from my pay.

That Friday night came, and my roommate and I were there. I had on a long, red, cuddly velvet robe that had been a Christmas gift from my parents. I had on underneath it my underwear and my nightgown, and I had on my socks and my bunny-fur house shoes—like a little kid about to have her tonsils out. And I was terrified.

He showed up at midnight. He had on a black overcoat. He had the whitest, pastiest face I've ever seen, with large pock marks, and his fingernails were dirty—I remember that. He was an older man, not white-haired, kindly-looking; he looked like the kind of man your mother tells you not to speak to in the bus terminal.

He had a black bag, and he came in looking behind him at the door, looking all around. He said, "Where's the cash?" My roommate, being brave, said, "We're not going to pay you until this is done." He turned and walked right out the door. And so she ran down the hall and said, "Okay, okay," and he came back in.

We went into my bedroom, and he told me to leave on the red fuzzy robe but take off everything else. I asked him to turn his back, and I took off all my clothes underneath my robe. I lay down on my little twin bed, and he gave me a shot, which he said was sodium pentothal, and he made me count backwards, told me I would wake up in about an hour or so, and that I might be thirsty, and that I would be bleeding, and that was all.

He did not tell me, and I did not know, how dangerous it is to give sodium pentothal to somebody under that kind of condition. You might not ever come out of it. If anything goes wrong, you don't have an anesthesiologist there, and this is a very strong anesthesia—it puts you totally under. He did not give me a number to call if anything went wrong. He did not tell me I would be cramping. And he was not there when I woke up.

I have no memory of the procedure at all. I assume he gave me a D&C. It would be years later before I had any information about what different kinds of abortions were or anything like that. I recall the word "scrape" being used, which is a frightening word. When women finally did begin to talk, we found out how many of us went through this, and how many women were abused sexually under those circumstances. I have a sense, I suppose, that it was a blessing that I was out cold, although that was very dangerous.

My roommate was there when I woke up. I was cramping. I was bleeding, as he'd said, but we didn't know how much was normal. So we sat up that night drinking tea and trying to do those exercises for cramps that they had taught us in gym class, which of course didn't work. I was scared to death, not knowing whether I was okay or whether I was dying.

Well, I was okay physically. I did not die. And I lived to have two wonderful children. I did get married again in 1968—I went back home and married the boy next door, basically—and the first thing I did was set out to get pregnant. In some way, I wanted to atone for many things—for the abortion, partly, but also for having disappointed my parents and my friends and relatives and *me* in my failure at my first marriage. I wanted to prove to everybody that I could be a good wife and mother. That marriage lasted four years; I settled for one out of two.

My daughter was born in '69, and I had my son a year after that. You would think by this time I would have known more about birth control, and I did, but there was still quite a lot that I did not know. The doctor told me when I had my daughter that if I were nursing her and using the foam, I couldn't get pregnant. I went back to him for my three-month checkup after my daughter was born, and the doctor said, "Well, you're in great shape— and congratulations, you're pregnant again!"

Now, I really did not want another child then; I had a three-month-old. I had not lost the weight yet, my husband and I were not making a lot of money, and it was all we could do to support one child and ourselves. But I chose to have my son. I don't know that it had anything to do with the abortion. Certainly that's never been far from my mind. No woman comes away clean from an abortion, even if you come away clean physically. I've said over and over that I am not for abortion, that no one is for abortion. I am for a woman's right and a man's right—I'm for your right to make your own hard choices in this world.

I think that one of the things that makes me angriest, as angry as the shame and the pain I had to go through for the illegal abortion, is the lack of education, of sex education in the home, in the church, in the school, all of those places that didn't give me any information that got me into that place. The same people who don't want you to have an abortion don't want you to have sex education, and there is no question where this ignorance leads. And anyone who thinks that outlawing abortion makes abortion go away is a fool. It makes it uneconomical, it makes it dangerous, and it makes it shameful.

I had another abortion later on, a legal abortion, because there was some damage to the child. It was a partial miscarriage, and I then had to complete it. Probably the child was dead already, that was the best guess, and if not, the child was malformed.

I was in my late thirties, and I wanted the child. Anytime I could have had a baby in the last two years, I would have. If I got pregnant, even inadvertently and unmarried, I would have had the child. I could afford to support one, and I'm competent to raise one—although that might be debatable; ask my children. That abortion was hard to recover from; I found out then that it was my last chance, that what was wrong physically would be that way with other pregnancies.

But having the legal abortion was so totally different from having the illegal one. It was inexpensive. It was done in a clinic, a Planned Parenthood clinic, under sterile circumstances, with counseling, and I was not made to feel worse than I already felt. I was helped in grieving my loss, and it was a loss. *Both* times it was a loss.

So I have seen it from all three sides—I have two living wonderful children, I had a legal abortion, and I had an illegal abortion. I am the mother of two or the mother of four, depending on how you look at it. I tend to look at it that I am the mother of two.

About the question "Does life begin at conception?"—I don't know. Life in a certain sense probably does begin at conception, even perhaps right before conception—the properties of life are in the sperm and they're in the womb. But one must make tough choices in this world, harder choices than abortion. I don't see that choice as any different from the choice that families and doctors always have to make in difficult childbirth when they can only save the mother or save the fetus: You go for the life that is.

Danitra Vance

Danitra Vance is a performance artist, actress, and comedian. She began her career at La MaMa ETC. and is best known for the stint she did as a *Saturday Night Live* regular during the 1985–86 season and for her roles in two plays produced by the Public Theater in New York City—*Spunk,* based on stories by Zora Neale Hurston, for which she won an Obie Award; and *The Colored Museum,* for which she received the NAACP Theatre Image Award.

A native of Chicago, Vance lives in Brooklyn. Her story, which she wrote for this collection, concerns her mother's abortion in the mid-sixties when Vance was five years old.

Strawberries, cherry pop, toy fire engines, red whips, red-hots, red gumballs, red Lifesavers . . . I didn't like anything red. If I tried to put on my red turtleneck by myself, it seemed to almost smother me.

One night, a few years ago, when Mom and I were having a heart-to-heart, she reminded me about the last time I saw my father. He'd buttoned me into a pretty new red coat. I guess, after that, I couldn't stand anything red. Until that conversation, I never knew why.

Some things you remember . . . some things you never forget.

I remember.

I was ready—fully equipped book satchel, pencils and erasers neatly organized in a snappy pencil box, notebook, paper, crayons. I believe I even had a protractor and a compass. Everything was new: My school supplies were new, my clothes were new, I was new, the school was new.

There was a huge polished wood door, and it had a big glass-and-wire window. I took a breath and walked into the classroom. My heart fell. Tables! A great big room with a few tables and little-kid-size chairs, baby chairs. Where were the desks? I asked. Mrs. Burchette told me to put my book bag on the windowsill and not to bring it again. She had only one book in the classroom.

Kindergarten . . . disappointing.

The only thing I really learned, the only skill, the only surprise, the only new accomplishment I could carry with me from this post-nursery-but-not-really-real-school school, the only thing I can say about kindergarten, is that I learned about milk.

I learned there were Mama, Papa, and Baby Bear sizes. I could choose brown or white milk. The brown milk wasn't white milk diluted with Bosco or Hershey's or "O-val O-val O-valtine" or "N-E-S-T-L-E-S, Nestles makes the very best . . . chocolate." Brown milk was chocolate milk. It came that way, no fuss, nor stirring, like a brown cow made it. Hurrah, a revelation. I followed the teacher's instructions and opened my pint-sized carton of already colored, already flavored chocolate milk. Some cartons were easy, some cartons more of a challenge. Some days I forgot to look for the little arrows and opened the back of the little roof instead of the front, and the spout wouldn't pop out.

One day I got up the courage to tell my grandmother, who we lived with, that I didn't want to go to school anymore. She sang,

"Or would you rather be a mule? A mule is an animal . . . he can't write his name or read a book . . . or would you like to swing on a star, carry moonbeams home in a jar." What she sang made a lot of sense. I didn't want to be a mule and, yeah, I'd like to swing on a star.

Then my grandmother and grandfather went away on one of those Indian summer vacations to "Ida While," wherever that was. They left me and my little sister alone with Mommy, for the first time.

I can't remember every detail, but Mommy got really, really sick. She was upstairs in bed in Gramma and Granddaddy's room. I was downstairs daydreaming, wishing I was old enough to be a Brownie. "Dee-Dee," my mother called. I climbed the stairs.

My little sister was on the bed. She comforted Mommy by placing her three-year-old hands on Mommy's face. "You're gonna be all right, Mommy," she said. Mommy didn't look so hot to me. She looked like she'd been crying.

I watched my mother and my sister. They fascinated me— nursing, feeding, kissing, cuddling, talking. My sister was the baby. I was grown; I was five. I didn't need training wheels on my bike. I didn't need all that lovey-dovey babified stuff.

"Dee-Dee, will you bring me some milk?" said my mother, asking me to perform a task she had not taught me or ever seen me do. Luckily, everything I needed to know about milk cartons I had learned recently. Oh boy. It was a half gallon. It was in the refrigerator above my head. It would be heavy—it hadn't been opened. I was determined.

The next day or maybe the day after that, sitting in the dark, I remember thinking, This must be how children in China and India feel. I have never been this hungry before. This must be what it feels like to starve. I need a CARE package.

I remember kneeling by the cocktail table wishing my mother wouldn't be sick, hoping she wouldn't go away like people do when they die.

She didn't.

• • •

Twenty years passed.

The family drove from Chicago to Danville, Virginia, for a funeral. On the way we stopped at a motel. I shared a bed with my mother, and we had one of those rare mother-daughter teen talks; a girl-giggle, truth-or-dare, grown-up slumber party; a whispering all-night discussion. She told me about the months leading up to my complicated premature birth. We talked about our memories of her divorce. That's the night she told me about the red coat. Then I told my mother about being hungry and thinking she was going to die.

"You *know* why"—a statement, not a question—"don't you?"

"If I didn't know then, how could I know now?" I asked her.

"I had to wait for Mother and Daddy to leave, so I could have it done, you know."

I didn't know, and I let her know I didn't know by saying nothing.

"I had an abortion."

I was supposed to guess that? Me, who was shocked to find birth control pills in my mother's purse when I was in high school? I always wanted to believe my mother was Donna Reed. My mother was more a combination of Lana Turner, Gidget, and Carmen Jones.

My mother told me there was no way she could have had that baby. She was in the middle of a divorce. She was just twenty-four. She couldn't afford it—financially, emotionally, intellectually, spiritually, physically.

When she realized she was pregnant, she didn't know where to go or what to do. Weeks passed. She tried overdoses of laxatives, throwing herself off the stairs, adding secret potions to burning hot baths. Then she found a nurse.

She described the place she went to, and it made me think of the unfurnished room where Natalie Wood didn't have the abortion in *Love with the Proper Stranger*, and the place where the white girl did have the abortion in *In the Heat of the Night*. Dim, dingy room, single exposed light bulb hanging from the ceiling, table covered with newspaper, unrecognizable "surgical" instruments. They put a catheter inside her body and packed her with gauze.

Then she came home and waited for "it" to happen. In those days the pregnancy was eventually terminated by the woman herself.

She had horrible pains, then maneuvered herself to the bathroom. She pushed and pushed and pushed out clot after clot, squeezing and forcing and pressing with all her strength. When she thought her body had recovered enough to return to bed, she rose, glanced down, and saw the umbilical cord dangling between her legs.

"I thought I was going to lose my mind," she told me. "I didn't see anything else. Nobody had told me what to expect or what to do. I had enough sense to keep pushing, to get everything out. I knew you and your sister were in the house, and Mother and Daddy were away. I knew I couldn't let anything happen. But I couldn't stop the bleeding. I had your sister bring me the pads they had given me. I called you and asked you to get me some milk."

A five-year-old and a three-year-old kept their mother alive.

When Gramma and Granddaddy returned from the vacation, I couldn't stand to be away from them. If Gram got a cold and had to stay in bed, I cried. If they both went for a drive or to the store without me, I became hysterical. I'd chase the car until someone came back to stay with me. I had always been a level-headed little girl. Now I had uncontrollable, unreasonable fears.

After one of those car-chasing/crying episodes, they both got out of the car. I thought they were going to put me out of my misery, and they did. They showed me there was plenty of food, gave me some, and promised to return very soon. They looked at me like they were hugging me—I didn't like to be hugged, that was for babies. They looked at me like they loved me.

How could they still love me when obviously I was crazy? How could they understand me when I didn't understand me or this bizarre behavior? Gram rubbed some tears off my round, brown face, and Granddaddy covered my face with his great big hands. I stopped crying.

It's funny, until I wrote this piece, I had never fit these elements together. I was one of those children overly concerned about death and abandonment and food, and it was all mixed up. I never understood any of it . . . until today.

Margot Kidder

Actress Margot Kidder is most familiar to American audiences as the legendary Lois Lane in the Superman movies; she has starred also in such films as Paul Mazursky's *Willie and Phil.* Lately Kidder has moved behind the camera, as resident director at the Center for Advanced Film Studies in Toronto, where she made a documentary about turning forty in a society that refuses to let women grow old.

At forty-two, Kidder makes her home in upstate New York, on the banks of the Hudson. Three times divorced, she lives with her fifteen-year-old daughter, Maggie, whom she raised alone after her divorce from novelist Thomas McGuane.

The world of mining camps is not only cold and not only isolated and not only rough, but it is very masculine. Women don't have a prayer. Daddy was a miner. My mother, being a terribly bright, onetime ambitious woman, had the misfortune of being born into that generation that demanded you do what your husband wanted you to do. She instilled in me and my sister a very strong understanding of the need to be independent, to think for ourselves.

Because a great deal of my childhood was spent in and around northern Quebec, which at that time was completely dominated by the Catholic church, the church got a finger in the soup of my brain. My parents weren't very religious, so I didn't get it in the home as much as from outside, from friends at school and going to church. But I seem to have grown up with all of the guilt and double standards associated with Catholicism.

My relationship with my mother had been pretty volatile in my teenage years, and I had always been defiantly self-reliant. I was out of the house very young. I did a year at the University of British Columbia at sixteen, then I was gone. I went to Toronto to be an actress, and there I met a man who became my Henry Higgins. This fellow—we'll call him "John"—was quite a bit older than I; I was just eighteen, he was thirty-something. He was a wonderful, caring, sweet person. We lived in Montreal, and I was quite in love.

I wasn't on any birth control. I do remember going on the Pill at perhaps sixteen and feeling sick immediately, so I stopped taking it and lived in a state of irresponsible delusion about the possible consequences. I remember one day walking up to the top of Mount Royal in Montreal and feeling very dizzy and very ill, and having to go home and lie down. I had no idea what was wrong with me. This went on for several weeks. Finally, it dawned on me that I might be pregnant.

My sister had been born in Montreal, and I knew that the doctor who delivered her lived there. I found him in the phone book and very nervously went to his office and was examined by him and told I was about six weeks pregnant. It was stunning news to me.

On some level, I knew that having a baby would mean the end to everything I'd wanted since I was nine. I have diaries from back then saying, "I'm going to Hollywood to be a movie star." I was ambitious and determined. I don't know where I got it, because I'd grown up in mining camps in small northern towns and seen only two movies by the age of nine, but it was there. Besides, I wasn't emotionally mature enough to see that a baby would add to my life. I wasn't capable of that kind of love at that age.

I remember sitting down and saying to the doctor, "I can't have this baby. I have to have an abortion." And he became very angry and very cold, and said, "You know that's against the law. I don't want to talk about it." I went back to him a second time, pleading, and he said, "Go ask someone in a drugstore." That's how ignorant I was: I went from drugstore to drugstore in Montreal asking the chemists in French and in English how I could get an abortion.

It never occurred to me to go to my mother or my father; I didn't really communicate with them about that sort of thing. I had no women friends I could ask. So finally I told John. He was stunned as well but wanted the child, although he was wise and wonderful enough to understand that a barely eighteen-year-old girl who doesn't want to have a baby should not be forced to have the baby—he was a bit ahead of most other men of his time. He asked a lot of his friends and finally found out about a woman in Toronto. He made the appropriate phone calls. It was all done with great secrecy and a great sense of evil and sordidness.

We checked into the hotel in Toronto, and I wept and wept and was extremely nervous. The doorbell rang, and a woman who looked like an aging hooker—possibly she was—with false eyelashes and a lot of makeup on, came to the door. We talked for a bit, and I was clutching John's hand and feeling terrified. She insisted that no matter what happened, under no conditions was I to go to a hospital, under no conditions was I to call the police, under no conditions was I to give out her name. We promised not to betray her.

John was heartbroken, wrenched from top to bottom over this. He loved me very much, and he wanted to have the child, but he was doing what he knew was right for me, or what we thought was right. I think he paid her whatever the money was.

I was told to undress and lie in the bathtub, which I did. John was in the other room. There was no anesthetic, of course. She jammed something through my cervix. It was incredibly painful. I was screaming and crying; I had no idea what was happening to me. Then she used what looked like a douche to shoot some sort of solution up through my cervix. When it was over, I remember lying in the bathtub weeping in pain and overhearing a mumbled conversation in the other room between the woman and John, and then she left.

John came in and took me in his arms and put me in bed and explained to me that I was going to go through a lot of pain, but eventually the fetal matter would come out, and I would be fine. I was told to take some pills she'd given us for the pain; we didn't even ask what they were.

I began to go into labor, incredibly horrific pain for I don't know how many hours—ghastly, ghastly pain. I was screaming and clutching John and sobbing and didn't know what was happening. And yet we had made a pact that under no condition would we go to a hospital; we felt we should honor it, for her sake. So I ate the pills she'd given me, which didn't do anything. The pain continued, I was bleeding, I kept passing out.

Finally, John said, "I don't care what happens to us; we're going to the hospital." I don't remember how I got there, in an ambulance, a taxi. I barely remember getting into the emergency ward, being rushed on a stretcher somewhere, and then I was out. When I came to—I don't know how many hours later—a doctor and a nurse came in, and they looked very scornfully at me, the nurse with a bit of pity. I was told that I had almost died, that the woman had filled me full of Lysol.

I remember beginning to weep because it seemed to me that I had done a terrible, terrible thing. If you combine the secrecy, and the illegality, and the disapproval, and the desire of the father to have the child, the guilt was horrendous. I wept for what would have been a baby, and I remember saying, "I want my baby back." I wept and wept and wept. It didn't occur to me to feel sorry for *myself*, for what *I* had been through. This is the world, I thought: You take the action, you pay the price. And I paid very dearly.

Subsequently the nightmares began, the most horrible, horrible nightmares. They were constant and went on for a long time—images of children running at me with slashed wrists, of dead babies, of hunks of stuff coming out of my vagina. The nightmares were all colored in the same feeling of sin. The message was: You're terrible. You're a bad person. There is nothing about you that's redeemable. You are condemned to live in hell forever.

It haunted me and scarred me deeply. A liberating thing was being able to make something creative out of that experience in a film I did at the American Film Institute's Women's Directing Workshop when I was twenty-four. I'd written a long speech at the end of the piece where the main character I created talks about just this abortion. There was relief in telling the secret.

The nightmares stopped when I had my child, which was when I was twenty-seven years old.

In spite of the emotional confusion I lived through and the nightmares, I did not regret the abortion. I cried for the loss. I went through the grief. But I always knew I would not have been a good mother then. I knew that having that baby would have been wrong for the baby, and that you don't do that to children.

Abortion might be killing a life; I don't know. That to me is not an issue. If there is a sin, it is the sin that we adults perpetrate on the children of the earth who truly are innocent and defenseless by bringing those children into the world when they will not be cared for. To me, nothing justifies that sin. There are all over the globe children starving, being raped, dying, being beaten up because they're unwanted. They suffer abuses from which they never recover, and they break my heart.

If we are to take any responsibility for our own lives as women, we've got to recognize that it's we who have to pay for the folly of becoming pregnant irresponsibly, not the children that might be born because of that folly. The emotional trauma and pain of an abortion—and there's no doubt for myself that it's there—should be borne by me rather than a lifetime of trauma being borne by a child. It's not just a child in Harlem who has no food on the table or clothing I'm talking about; it's also about a child of rich parents if the parents don't want it.

I wanted my daughter desperately. When I was twenty, twenty-one, I'd been told I couldn't have a baby because of the abortion and because of a Dalkon Shield, which I'd had in for a couple of years before it made me very sick and had to be taken out. They wouldn't even examine me. They'd say, "Ah, Dalkon Shield, illegal abortion? You can't have kids. Have a hysterectomy." My daughter's father and I went to fertility doctors, we did everything. The point is that my child was terribly wanted.

I finally told my daughter about my illegal abortion a few years ago. It was right after the pro-choice march on Washington. We were supposed to go to the march together and had great plans, but then I was unable to go because I was directing a film in Canada. I was very disappointed, and she, surprisingly to me, was very disappointed, too. But we talked. During those discussions, she kept calling it "pro-abortion," and I kept saying, "No, Maggie, it's pro-choice," and we would have long conversations about the difference, which is very important.

I'm not pro-abortion . . . because abortion hurts. It's emotionally painful. I am pro-*choice*—that being the choice of the mother, choice over my own body—because ultimately it's my womb, my nine months and the child I have to nurture . . . whether we like it or not, 99.9 percent of the time, women bring up the children. It's the choice to have or not have a child—to have is very much a part of pro-choice.

Anne Archer

Daughter of actress Marjorie Lord *(Make Room for Daddy)* and actor John Archer, Anne Archer is a stage and screen actress who has starred in a host of motion pictures. She is perhaps best known for her Oscar-nominated performance as the resilient wife in *Fatal Attraction* and for her more recent role opposite Harrison Ford in *Patriot Games.* In 1993, she will be seen in *Body of Evidence* with Madonna and Willem Dafoe and in Robert Altman's *Short Cuts.* Her other film credits include *Narrow Margin* with Gene Hackman, *Eminent Domain* with Donald Sutherland, and *Love at Large* with Tom Berenger. She also co-produced *Waltz Across Texas* with her husband and co-star, Emmy Award–winning sports producer/director Terry Jastrow. Archer and Jastrow live in Los Angeles with their sons, Tommy and Jeffrey.

Archer has taken a highly visible role on the pro-choice stage as well, serving as the first National Public Advocacy Chair for the Planned Parenthood Federation of America.

I remember driving with my boyfriend for thirteen or fourteen hours solid, to get from Los Angeles to Yuma, Arizona. We were afraid that if we left while school was in session, we would be suspect, so we planned the trip for over the Thanksgiving holiday. I told my mother I was going to spend the vacation with my boyfriend's family. Knowing I would need to rest after the abortion, we got a cheap motel room where we could stay the night.

The roads turned to dirt the minute we got across the Mexican border. Finally, we came to this little town, with all dirt roads—I think it was called San Luis Rey. I had been told the abortion was going to be performed in a hospital. We pulled up in front of this old building—you know that turquoise Mexican color buildings are painted? It was war-torn and falling apart, anything but what I expected a hospital to be. It was an old building that had been sort of makeshifted to perform abortions. We went inside and someone who appeared to be a nurse took me into this small, cramped room. There were metal bunk beds with blankets on them up against three walls, and there were girls on all the beds. It was warm in the room and looked grungy. I didn't feel the sheets were dirty, but the blankets were like old army blankets that you just didn't want to touch. They told me to take my clothes off, put on a robe, and lie down on one of the beds. That was the last I saw of my boyfriend until that evening.

I was in my second year of college at the time and nineteen years old; it was before abortion became legal. I'd gone to a Christian Science elementary school, an all-girls' high school, and then off to an all-girls' college. I'd dated a little bit. Then I met this very nice boy, and we started going together. He was the first boy I slept with, and I became pregnant the first time I had sex. He told me that foam was just as protective as the Pill. I completely believed him—he was my total source of information.

I had one close girlfriend at the time who I trusted would keep the silence with me, and she really is the person in the long run who saved my life. She found out through someone about a board for therapeutic abortions in the United States that disseminated information about where one could get an illegal therapeutic abortion. My boyfriend contacted the board, and they gave us the name of a doctor in Mexico.

Before I went for the abortion, that girlfriend came up with some pills that were supposed to abort. They looked like vitamin E. I took *all* of them. I was desperately hoping they would work, but nothing happened. Time passed, and when we finally got the name of the doctor in Mexico, I was about two and a half months pregnant—it could have been bordering on twelve weeks. It was a hard thing to judge because I had so little information and was afraid to discuss it with anyone.

Because I had grown up a Christian Scientist—a religion I loved—we seldom used the traditional medical-care system. I'd never had any medical tests, shots, or medications. I never needed them; I'd always been wonderfully healthy.

To find out if I was indeed pregnant, I went to a doctor. I went to a woman because I was too embarrassed to go to a man. She made me feel like dirt, and when she told me the results of the test were positive, I thought that meant I was okay and not pregnant. But I still didn't feel right, so I went to the school infirmary, even though I was very embarrassed to be seen walking in; I thought everyone would know why I was there.

Though I had seldom been to a doctor, I naively trusted doctors completely. When I went for my abortion, I was totally trusting. I'd not had any prior *bad* medical experiences, so I didn't worry that anything negative could happen. I knew I was going to a facility where the people were older, to a doctor, to this place where this was done all the time. But, in fact, we just got a doctor's name and all of a sudden were driving to the place; there was no way to check up on anything. It's only when I look back that I realize what a dangerous thing I did.

A nurse came into the little room and gave me a shot; I have no idea what it was. That was the first shot I'd ever had. No one knew what I might be allergic to, and I was so unaccustomed to any kind of medication that it almost knocked me out. I felt like I was suffocating. I couldn't even lift myself up off the bed.

No one checked on me to be sure I was okay. The next thing I knew I was put on a gurney and wheeled out. I remember feeling sick to my stomach, obviously from the medication; I thought I was going to throw up.

I was wheeled out through the reception area where there were fathers and other people—I don't remember seeing my boyfriend, I was too groggy—and into an operating room. I remember seeing a man in an operating gown and people around, someone putting my legs up in stirrups and a gas mask on my face, and feeling that I couldn't breathe.

I woke up as they were wheeling me back into that room. I think I threw up on the way. I must have slept there that entire day because we had gone in early that morning, and when they finally said I could go home, it was dark outside. When I got up, I couldn't walk very well.

I remember they brought me back into the reception area, and I sat down to wait while my boyfriend went to get the car. There was a father sitting there whose daughter was either having an abortion at that moment or had just had one. And I, from the medication, was feeling—now that it was over and done and successful—warm and all right with the world and kind of emotional and relieved and communicative. I said to him, "Don't worry, she'll be fine. It's going to be okay." He looked at me disapprovingly and said, *"I don't know what's the matter with you girls today."* I remember being devastated and humiliated. It was terrible. That man in that waiting room was a daddy to me, protecting his daughter, until then; today I know he was a cold human being who had no understanding of women. It had a terrific impact on me. . . .

Afterwards, I was bleeding heavily. They said I'd bleed for several hours. They gave me sulfa pills. That was one of the reasons that we had gone there, because they had an antibiotic to prevent infection.

My boyfriend got the car, and we drove back across the border. The poor guy never realized the pressure he'd been under. He had been so worried about me, it had been such a frightening thing. He felt so responsible. He'd had six hundred dollars in his savings account; I had nothing. The abortion cost everything he had. He hadn't eaten for almost a week, he'd been so anxious. We drove to our motel, where we had this big cardboard box full of food. I remember the dearest thing, my boyfriend kept opening these canned goods and he ate—I don't know how he could have eaten as much as he did—he just ate and ate. He was so exhausted that he lay down on the bed and went out like a light.

I had a very different night. I had a lot of cramping; I was in pain. And I went through an emotional ordeal, with a lot of postpartum feelings. I cried most of the night in the bathroom. I couldn't wake my boyfriend up and ask for comfort because he was just too exhausted. I went through it alone that night. I didn't regret the abortion. I've never had any regrets about not having that child, not even remotely; I knew it was right. And I had no problems conceiving after that, so the abortion probably was done correctly. But I had enormous emotional sadness over just having had to go through this clandestine thing. It was terrible.

I had that abortion because I viewed having a child at that time as an end to my life. All of my hopes and dreams for myself would have had to be put aside. I had planned and worked hard all my life to be an actress. While I loved my boyfriend, I certainly didn't feel ready to make the major decision that this was the boy with whom I should spend the rest of my life. And I know now that I certainly wasn't emotionally ready to give the full-time attention and nurturing to a young child that each and every one so rightly deserves.

Telling my mother that I was pregnant at the time was not an option. I was afraid that she would be so worried about the dangers of the abortion that I'd have to have the baby; she would have feared for my health. But I think more than that, I didn't want her to know that I'd gotten pregnant. She would have understood, but I would have had to see the look on her face when she first found out, and I couldn't stand that.

Now I understand—then, I probably knew it, too—that my mother and my grandmother, who lived with us, would have taken total responsibility. But that would have been the horror of all horrors; that would have put me under their thumb. I was just getting free—I was alone off at college, I was starting my life, I had goals. I would truly have gone backwards. It was a devastating thought to me. There was no way I would have had that baby. I *had* to get an abortion. I probably would have self-aborted with a coat hanger before I would have had that child.

I grew up, actually, in a very loving environment. My mother and my grandmother raised me because my mother and father divorced when I was four. My mother was the one who supported the family. I talked about love and relationships with my mother on end. The actual graphic details of the sexual act I don't think were ever discussed; she was probably shy about that.

My grandmother took care of us when my mother was working. She was very funny, with a terrific sense of humor and great wit. She could be rather outrageous at times, yet she was also very Victorian. She had a great effect on me. Even though she didn't say it directly, there was some feeling that sex was a little bit dirty. She felt very strongly that a woman should not allow herself to be used by a man and that girls who had sex and weren't married, or who were too available to men, were "sluts." She would never have used that word; they were not "ladies," is what she would say, but that was the implication. Though I felt those mores, common in society, were primitive and wrong, I still wanted society's—and my grandmother's— approval.

For me, being unmarried and pregnant was humiliation to the nth degree. I'm amazed at how, on a subtle level, the old-fashioned feelings were the ones that ruled. My friends were very liberal. We were women's libbers at the time. I believed that abortion should be legal, and sex before marriage was absolutely right, that it was a natural, human experience. But I also judged myself by the standards of my upbringing.

Years later, my mother and I took a trip to Hawaii. Up until then, my abortion had been a big secret in my life. My oldest son was three or four years old, and my first husband and I were getting a divorce. I was going through a very difficult time emotionally, and I had gotten some counseling help. I learned a great deal about myself; I learned that my secrets were not good for me.

My mother and I took my little boy to Hawaii with us, and we had the most wonderful time. One night—and I knew consciously I was going to do this—I sat down with my mother. I wanted to tell her all the things I'd always been afraid to tell her. Funny, I can cry about this . . . I told her lots of things about my marriage and why it had gone wrong, things about my early life, and about my first boyfriend and my abortion. She looked at me, smiled, and said, "Anne, I knew about your abortion." I asked her, "How could you know?" She said, "When you left and got married, I was cleaning out your room and found a letter that a girl in college had written you. She had gotten pregnant and knew you had had an abortion. She thought you might know where she could get one."

I didn't ask my mother why she never said anything to me, because I knew. She felt it would have been an invasion of my privacy to say she had read a letter of mine. I think she also felt that, if I didn't want to talk about it, she would honor that.

But as I told my story, she was extremely supportive. I could see that it was hard for her to hear that her daughter had gone through such a painful experience. She never said anything about what I should or shouldn't have done. She never said she wished I had told her, though I'm sure she did. There were no regrets; there was just love.

I don't think I was conscious of it at the time, but looking back, my abortion was a very important experience for me. I remember that at the time it outraged me that anyone could tell me what was going to happen to my body, that I was going to have to bear a child. I felt that was like a rape. I feel very strongly about a woman's right to control her body.

I also feel very strongly about the need for sex education. If I had been informed, I would never have used foam, and I would have already seen a gynecologist because the truth of the matter is I *was* going to have sex; my boyfriend and I had planned it. That's the thing people don't realize. Girls are going to have sex. The puberty experience for a girl, just as it is for a boy, is so driving and so enormous that to abstain until marriage is not realistic. You can't tell the breasts not to grow; you can't tell the period not to come. Young girls' bodies are yearning for sex—to link up, to connect, to mate. They need education so they can handle that drive responsibly.

But no matter how responsible one is—I felt I was a pretty special young woman, doing everything right, conservative in my life-style: no drinking, no drugs, good academics, president of the student body—a woman can find herself pregnant and know she cannot have that child and will do anything to prevent it. Women need to know that abortion is an option because it may be the only way they feel they can go on with their lives.

Even more than the unfairness to women, though, is the unfairness to the unborn child. If a woman finds herself pregnant with her sixth child and her husband has just walked out on her, I think that child is going to have an unfortunate life. If a woman is desperate, she is not going to be the mother she should be. I've raised two children; I know what it's like to care for those little ones. You have to want them, love them, and be ready for them.

If you believe that man is a spirit, as I do, better the spirit of the child should wait and find another body, one that really wants the child to be there. It is better that children come into the world with some strength around them.

Patricia Tyson

Patricia Tyson is the former director of the Religious Coalition for Abortion Rights in Washington, D.C., her hometown. An outgrowth of the Clergy Consultation Service, the major underground network that referred women for abortions during the 1960s, RCAR is a unique coalition of thirty-four mainline Protestant, Jewish, and other faith groups that was formed in 1973. Its purpose, says Tyson, is "to educate folks around the diversity within the religious community on the issue of choice, and to assure that no one theological perspective gets put into secular law."

Tyson, forty-five, is a longtime community and women's rights activist who helped to found the National Black Women's Political Congress. She lives in Washington with her husband, Tony Harrison, former state representative to the Alabama legislature from Birmingham, and their two sons.

When I took this job as director of RCAR in 1989, I didn't think about my personal experience with abortion. It had nothing to do with my taking the job, and I had no intention of letting anybody know about it.

What happened was, a lady from the *Today* show on NBC called here and asked me to help her find a woman of color who had had an illegal abortion. I said, "Let me call you back." I decided that I couldn't ask other women to share their experiences, to share their pain, if I wasn't willing to do it myself. Because there are only a few black women who head pro-choice groups, we need to be out there saying for other black women, for other women of color, "Yes, you can come out too. You can tell your stories, and I'll be there for you because I've had an abortion and spoken about it, and I understand how painful it is." I went on the show myself.

I think abortion has been a closet issue for us, more so than for white women. I can't see a black church coming out and saying, "I am pro-choice." There are no national Fundamentalist organizations in the Religious Coalition, no national Baptist organizations. I'm Baptist. I cannot see me being able to go to my minister and tell him that I have decided to terminate a pregnancy, and ask him for guidance or assistance, without his saying to me, "Oh, no. You can't do that." There has been an absence of support within the black religious community. It hasn't made black women comfortable in being able to go there when faced with an unwanted pregnancy—irrespective of the reason for not wanting that pregnancy. And it's unfortunate, because what that does is to break the spiritual thread.

As far as abortion and religion go, I don't know whether God necessarily would think that abortion is okay. In the Bible, he's absent on the issue. I think abortion isn't right; it isn't wrong. It's not that simple. We make decisions based on the circumstances that we find ourselves in at any given time, and that's all in my opinion religion calls upon me to do. You do the best that you can and take responsibility for that decision. What I really do consider a sin is to have technology available and not have folks be able to avail themselves of it.

I was eighteen years old, and it was in '65, '66, somewhere around there, when I had an illegal abortion. I was dating this guy from the time I was fifteen until the time I was twenty-two, twenty-three. We dated all the way through high school and never had sexual intercourse at all. Finally, we decided that we should do that, and quite honestly, it was the blind leading the blind. He didn't know any more about sex than I did.

We used to drive fifty miles outside of the District of Columbia and rent an old hotel room. We would go into the hotel room, jump into bed, bang, bang, bang, and then get back up, wash ourselves off, and go home. It was pitiful.

We didn't use birth control. We were using withdrawal; that was the birth control that I thought was the best birth control for us. Like I said, we were the blind leading the blind. About a year after we started to have sex, I ended up getting pregnant.

He was on his way to Vietnam, and for some odd reason, we thought that probably the best thing to do was get married. That's what nice girls did; you got pregnant, and you got married. But then one of my two older sisters said, "Do you really want to do this? Do you really like him? Is he the man you want to spend the rest of your life with?"

Once I sat down and started thinking about that, I said, "No. Wait a minute. This is not what I want to do." I removed myself from fantasyland, which was that we'd run off and marry, and then, when he came back from Vietnam, we would live happily ever after, with two little children, a white picket fence, a two-car garage . . .

I thought about it, and I decided this was not for me, and it wasn't for him. We didn't know where we were going. I didn't know whether or not I really wanted him. And there were other things I wanted to do. I had gotten out of high school and started working at the Federal Aviation Administration in 1965 as a clerk stenographer, one of the few black women that came in at a GS3 rating, making all of ninety-one dollars every two weeks. I knew I'd like to go to school eventually and do something else.

I think that single teenage girls, black and white, who don't get pregnant and have babies—like my three nieces—don't do it because they see opportunity. My nieces decided very early in life, "I want to be a pharmacist; I want to be a lawyer; I want to be a psychologist." They viewed pregnancy as a deterrent to their dreams, and saw their dreams as attainable. My dreams were limited because I was a black female in this society at an earlier point in time, but I had dreams.

Because we had decided not to get married, I did not perceive having a baby by myself as an alternative in my situation. Nice middle-class girls during that time didn't have babies out of wedlock. You embarrassed your family; you embarrassed yourself; you became a slut for life, or whatever you want to call it.

I talked to my two older sisters. I think my sisters told my mom, but me and my mother have an unwritten agreement that we won't talk about it. We talked about it when I decided to go on the *Today* show, and that was it. She just said to me, "I don't remember." And that's okay, that's really okay. I don't need to force her to remember those things if she has decided not to remember.

We found an abortionist who was a salesclerk, a salesclerk in a dress shop, in Washington. I must have been maybe one or two months pregnant; it was fairly early. We went to her apartment, which was in southeast Washington, a nice place for recently married couples who saved their money and then moved on to better things. We went into the bedroom.

She used a speculum, the thing that allows a doctor to look into your vaginal cavity, and shot a red catheter into the uterus. Then she packed me with cotton, gauze, or something like that, to make sure that the tube stayed in place.

The only thing I wanted was for it to be over with. When it was, I gave her fifty dollars, and she proceeded to tell me what would happen—that probably within twenty-four hours, I would start bleeding. I should take out the gauze, the tube would come out, and along with the tube, the uterus in essence would empty itself.

Twenty-four hours later, I was bleeding and bleeding and bleeding some more at home in my bed. My mother helped me to the bathroom. It lasted for about twelve or thirteen hours, and

I stayed at home and slept. I stayed off my feet for a couple of days, and then I thought everything was fine, except I never stopped bleeding. I would have these massive blood clots; the whole process in essence would start again.

It was really terrible, but you know, when you don't know anything about your body, you keep thinking, Oh, it'll stop. It really will go away. But it didn't, and I was losing so much blood. Then, I either passed out or my blood went so low that I had to go to the hospital. I had to get blood transfusions.

The doctors told me that I had had an incomplete abortion [some tissue fragments were left inside]. On top of that, the uterus was scarred. They wanted to do a hysterectomy. My mother said, "No, no, she's too young." That's what they did to all the little "hot" girls during my time frame, in the sixties. When you were pregnant and unmarried and black, their first suggestion to you nine times out of ten was a hysterectomy. I also think they suggested a hysterectomy because it was a public hospital and my health insurance would have covered a hysterectomy, even though the hysterectomy was due to a botched abortion, but it would not cover a D&C that was abortion-related. They gave me a D&C.

The worst thing about the experience for me was that the woman who'd done the abortion had said to me, after she'd put the tube in, "If there are any problems, don't call me." You felt like a piece of meat on the rack, you know? Nobody really cared about you. And that whole process was bad. You bled all over the place. It was not a good process at all.

That was the worst part—that, and not being able to say it to anybody, acting like it didn't happen, not being able to talk about it, even among those individuals who knew. When I went into the hospital, my two older sisters and my mother knew. My dad, my two younger sisters, and my two brothers didn't know; they were told I had a kidney infection or something like that.

I think there were certain things that my mother felt comfortable in telling them—certain things that it was correct to tell folks at that point in time.

One thing that experience with abortion taught me—and one reason why I carry my own name today—is it said to me very clearly, "You ain't got to depend on no dude to take care of you. That is a fantasy." The man wasn't there. He wasn't in Vietnam yet, but he was not there. He was not the one who came up with the fifty dollars; he was not the one who walked up those steps with me; he was not the one who rushed me to the hospital. He came into the hospital later on with flowers thinking that everything was fine.

We never talked about it, and I went with this sucker until I was about twenty-two years old! I'd love to sit up here and tell you he was a bum, but he wasn't. He was not a bad guy. Today, he's a businessman, very successful, very nice, very smart. That was just what guys did at that time. It was always your problem; it wasn't their problem. You were the one who got pregnant because you were not careful. It was like it was an immaculate conception.

When my abortion was over, I wanted to forget it. I really did. It was not something you wanted to think about. Some people don't understand the anxiety that women like myself had. Women who find themselves with an unwanted pregnancy will do anything in order to make themselves whole again. I don't think people understand the power of that force, of that drive to be whole. Who in the world who did not feel like a cornered rat would go to a saleswoman for an abortion? Think about that. I knew when I walked up those steps to her apartment that something might happen, and I might not walk back down. I knew that. But I also knew that was the only choice I had.

W h o o p i   G o l d b e r g

Performance artist, screen star, and television actress Whoopi Goldberg, whose real name is Caryn Johnson, was born in 1955 in Manhattan. She began performing at the age of eight in New York City; as a teenager joined the choruses of such shows as *Hair*, *Jesus Christ Superstar*, and *Pippin*; and at nineteen, with one-year-old daughter Alexandrea from her first marriage, headed for California, where she performed in such ensembles as the San Diego Repertory Theatre, Spontaneous Combustion, and, in partnership with David Schein, the Blake Street Hawkeyes Theatre in San Francisco.

In California, Whoopi began to develop the repertoire of characters who eventually peopled her resoundingly successful one-woman Broadway show, which she later recorded, earning a Grammy. An Oscar-nominated, Golden Globe Award—winning performance as Celie in *The Color Purple* launched her film career; she later won the Academy Award for Best Supporting Actress for her portrayal of wisecracking psychic Oda Mae Brown in *Ghost.*

Twice divorced and living in Los Angeles, Whoopi is now a grandmother. Her first grandchild, Amarah Skye Martin, was born in 1989 on November 13—Whoopi's birthday.

I grew up in Chelsea, in a housing project on Twenty-sixth Street, Tenth Avenue. We were a mixture, a bunch of mutts—Jews, Catholics, all kinds of other weird stuff.

My mother sent me to Catholic school, for a better education, I guess. They considered me Catholic, but I only considered myself Catholic because I went to Catholic school. I didn't believe a lot of the things they said. An angry God was not the one I felt I knew. I believed in a kinder God than the one they were talking about.

Sex was never mentioned in school, God no. My mom—who was a nurse—was pretty up front. She said, "This is how babies were made." Period. Very clinical. Nothing about the fun stuff. I didn't know about birth control when I was a kid. I didn't learn about it until well into my teens.

I first had sex at thirteen, it was 1968. That seems young only if you thought about it as "sex." It was "It." I was doing "It."

I found out I was pregnant when I was fourteen. I didn't get a period. I talked to nobody. I panicked. I sat in hot baths. I drank these strange concoctions girls told me about—something like Johnny Walker Red with a little bit of Clorox, alcohol, baking soda—which probably saved my stomach—and some sort of cream. You mixed it all up. I got violently ill.

At that moment I was more afraid of having to explain to anybody what was wrong than of going to the park with a hanger, which is what I did. Probably I was afraid to admit that I had had sex, because, remember, the Catholics said you only did it when you were married, and then only in the dark, and here I'd done it in the light in some hallway. But I also didn't grow up around young unmarried girls having kids.

I went to the dry cleaners and got a hanger. I took it to the park in Chelsea because it was close and had a bathroom. There wasn't a lot of traffic in and out. I didn't do it at home because parents are funny—when you want them to go away, they go, and then they come right back. It was just a private thing, something I needed to do. I never thought I was going to die; young people never think they're going to die. It seemed very simple at the time: You just do that, and it goes away.

The worst thing was not knowing what I was doing, really. You could go to the library and find out all kinds of information about how women took care of themselves. I read these stories by a health worker on the Lower East Side. She'd find these girls who'd been to these butchers, then have to doctor them up afterwards. She described the various methods women used and how awful it was. A hanger was the convenient thing.

I didn't bleed a ton, but some, so I cleaned up a little, and rinsed out my underwear like a good girl. Afterwards, I was in a lot of pain. I think the hanger worked, 'cause I then had a period several days later. God was with me—knock on wood—I punctured nothing; I didn't completely destroy my body. But I have a bad body; I have a sensitive body. Whenever I go to the gynecologist, any probing is very painful; it's always been that way.

The character in my show, the thirteen-year-old Valley Girl who self-aborts, uses a hanger, too. The rest of her story has very little to do with me. I was not the kind of girl that I'm portraying. She's rejected by everybody. The priest sends her to the nun, the nun sends her home, and on the way home she meets a friend who tells her about the concoction I used. After she drinks it, she throws herself down the stairs and that doesn't work, then she goes and tells her mom, who throws her out. She goes to the library, as I did, and because the information is much more available—information on techniques that people use, now in manuals—she gets the information and does it.

One of the things she describes is the hooking of the top of the hanger, which I wish I had known about. Sometimes, what they would do is straighten the hanger, like I did, and then loop and twist one end, so that when they put that end inside, they didn't get the perforation. She uses the loop. In the show, I do it very slow because I want the audience to understand what we're talking about: We're talking about a wire metal hanger with one end that is looped and twisted and then inserted in the vagina, up into the uterus, and moved around. Being the space cadet that she is, she loops it but doesn't twist the end all the way down. That's why she has so much trouble with it; she in fact just tears out the interior of her uterus and hemorrhages.

I made the character white because nobody would have given a fuck about a poor woman of color—that's the bottom line. I wanted the people I knew were coming to my shows to see *their* children, to see and relate to *their* daughter. I hoped that putting it in that perspective—of somebody yelling for help and not being able to get it, somebody who looks a lot like your kid— would open people up, and they would listen more. I think I am too harsh to say that nobody would have given a fuck. They would have. I just don't think it would have been as effective to the people I was talking to, because then it would have become, "Oh, another black pregnant woman."

I cried a little bit at the time of that abortion, but not much. I was not a crier. I was like Mr. Peabody. I looked like a little light bulb with this little light bulb body and these eyes that sort of said, "And what's next?" I cry now sometimes when I think of it, when I think that I could have gone to my mother, as I discovered the following year. I could have saved myself a trip to the park with a hanger.

I had another abortion the next year, when I was fifteen. By then, it was 1970 and legal in New York. That decision was harder because I wasn't exactly sure I didn't want to have a baby, but my mother knew I didn't want to have a baby. She was great. She said, "*Look.* You can't do this now. There's too much you have to do." She was right. I knew I was not ready for a child.

I hadn't been using birth control at that time. For one thing, I still didn't know where to go for it. And it was the late sixties; everybody was having sex. You had sex in Central Park; it was that free. Those were the good times—Cream was at the Fillmore, the Doors were at the Fillmore, all those cats. It was peace on earth, and balloons, and flowers, and a place for everybody, so people were having children left and right. I hate to call them the good times because I know they really weren't.

I think I went to Planned Parenthood for the abortion. They

gave me birth control, the Pill, and I started to use it, but I'm one of these people they haven't made contraception strong enough for. Always, I'm pregnant; you look at me and I'm having your kid. Three times, I got pregnant using birth control.

My daughter, who I had when I was eighteen and married, was a Pill baby. I had taken the Pill religiously, *religiously.* Then, I didn't get pregnant for a long time. I left my husband. I moved to California. I met a new man who had, like, sperm of doom. Every time this sperm of doom got near me, we were having kids. I got pregnant with him using a diaphragm and an IUD at the same time. I was twenty-five—this was around 1980. While I was still twenty-five, I got pregnant with him again, this time using some fucking European bullshit sponge; I could have cut a sponge from the supermarket and put it in there and put some cream on it and had the same effect. There are people out there who say, "Well, some birth control works for everybody." It's not true. My choice, when I discovered that this could become something that would happen a lot, was to have my tubes done. I did that when I was twenty-six.

I couldn't have those babies because it was not the time or the relationship. I was not prepared to take care of them, and it was not affordable at all. Those were tough times—I was on welfare for a while. Me and my daughter worried; we never knew we were worrying, but we were. Having a child and being on your own is tough. I was already raising one child, and my thought was, I don't want to be a single parent again.

The man and I had great discussions before I went for those abortions. I felt it was important for him to say whatever he had to say. But he understood that I was not prepared, and he was not prepared. One day, we hoped we would be, but unfortunately, our relationship didn't work out. But, yeah, we wept . . . we wept going for those abortions, we wept coming back . . . because both times this was something made from love.

I have a lot of trouble with people who accuse other people

of abusing abortion as a means of birth control. If abortion was something I was going to use as a method of birth control, then I would probably see a shrink. Anybody who's ever had an abortion knows it's not something you really want to do again. It's not like going to the hairdresser or getting your legs waxed. It's an agonizing decision and a very painful thing.

I had all my abortions in the early weeks. I don't feel that there is life in the first four weeks. Some scientists and other people will dispute that, but that's just my belief. People never know they're pregnant until after a month or two, so that first four weeks is sort of like *stuff* coming together.

I have a problem with second-trimester abortions because that's a person. You can look in those sonograms and see a person—there's a heartbeat; there's all kinds of stuff. I think the first two months is the time to have an abortion, if you're going to do it. With all the information around, most women would know before the third month that they're pregnant. To wait five or six months to decide to abort seems wrong to me. But that's only for myself. The reasons women have abortions vary, and there are many things to grapple with: Is it better to abort a child with Down's syndrome, or one you know will be born with AIDS? I don't know. That's why I'm for the decision being a personal one, without interference of government or special interest groups.

My daughter was fifteen when she had her baby. She chose to have a baby. It would not have been the choice I would have made for her; I think fifteen is young. But she had the choice, and she took it. I thought, It may be wonderful for her, so you stand behind her. A lot of parents don't stand behind their kids, which is why the laws don't allow parents to make this decision for their kids. For me, the laws are inconvenient, because I would have chosen for her to wait.

My daughter knew about birth control; she knew about safe sex; she knew about all that stuff. She didn't want to marry the man. But she wanted to have this baby. She was ecstatic about this baby, and this baby kicked all the time because it knew that there would be a lot of wonderful things waiting for it. She wasn't like the usual teenage mother who you see and think, Ah, poor baby. My daughter was phenomenal. She was one of those women who floated around.

Now, I'm Grandma Whoop. I think that I should be able to do some things better with my daughter's child than I could do with her. This kid is not going to have to worry about our next meal, for a little while anyway. Having some money takes a little pressure off, but I can't say it matters much on an emotional level. It's hard to be a mother; it's harder even when you're a kid.

My daughter made a choice that has changed her life and everyone else's life around her. She has hundreds of plans and none. Do I worry? All mothers do, whether their child is a mother or not. We do the best we can and hope for the best. She's not the first or the last young mother, and she knows she's not alone in it.

My commitment to choice comes from my belief that you have the right to decide whether you want to have children or not. The bottom line is that if someone does not want to have a child, they should not be forced into it. That's between the woman, her man if she chooses to make him aware, and God, whoever God is.

I talk about God because God and I are very close. God gives you choice—God gives you freedom of choice; that's in the Bible. God says, "Here are ten rules: Don't lie—you'll never remember what you said before; Don't cheat, because you're going to be mad if you're cheated on; Honor your parents, because they brought you into the world, and you're going to need child care. If you choose to live by them, your life will be better, and even if you don't, I will forgive you."

I have this deep belief that God understands whatever dilemma you're in and will forgive it if you make a choice that He or She doesn't think is right. That's *God's* prerogative. That's not Randall Terry's [founder of the militant anti-choice group Operation Rescue] prerogative. That's not George Bush's prerogative. That's not the Supreme Court's prerogative.

I read something a couple of weeks ago where Randall Terry expounded upon his belief of what a family should be—the wife, the child, and the place the woman has. I thought, Man, I want you to come marry *me*. He believes the man is the last word, and the woman should be seen and not heard. And I said: "Of course, this is not about whether abortion is right or wrong; this is about control."

The other thing, too, what would make it sort of a little bit easier, is if you could get some of these black and Puerto Rican and Chicano babies adopted. Nobody adopts these babies. They all want little white babies, cute white babies with blond hair and blue eyes. Why bring a child in that you know is going to spend its life in a fucking institution? What are those peoples' alternatives to *that*?

Women will always get abortions—black community, white community, Chicano community, Puerto Rican community; that will never stop. The issue is: Why can't they be safe and clean? What are you going to do, drag the woman to jail for sixty years for having an abortion?

My abortions didn't make me more radical. People's feelings against them made me more radical. I didn't talk about my abortions when I was a kid, but after I became a grown woman, I did. People weren't talking about their abortions at that time, but nobody looked like me either, so it was in keeping with me. People would say, "Oh, you did that?" And I'd say, "Yeah. But you liked me up until five minutes ago before you heard that, so obviously it didn't make me a nasty, horrible person, did it?"

Judy Widdicombe

As a registered nurse in St. Louis, Missouri, fifty-four-year-old Judy Widdicombe had a ringside seat in middle America during the days of illegal abortion. She has been a familiar figure on the front lines of the pro-choice battle for more than twenty-five years.

Widdicombe is founder and former president of Reproductive Health Services in St. Louis, named plaintiff in *Webster* v. *Reproductive Health Services*, the U.S. Supreme Court decision that paved the way for greater statewide efforts to regulate abortion than at any time since *Roe*. Widdicombe also helped to found the Missouri Clergy Consultation Service; the National Abortion Federation, which sets standards for abortion providers; and most recently, the Health Policy Institute, which advocates improved maternal and child health services. Voters for Choice, the National Abortion Rights Action League, and the Planned Parenthood Federation of America have assigned Widdicombe official posts at various times.

Widdicombe is the mother of five grown children, a grandmother, and a foster parent to substance-exposed infants. She makes her home in St. Louis.

I moved into the abortion issue in 1965 through a hotline I was doing volunteer work for—a suicide prevention hotline. In those days, there was no official place a woman with an unwanted pregnancy could go for help. So women would call us and say, "I'm desperate. I'm going to kill myself." We would try to encourage them to talk to their doctors and examine their situations to see if things were as bad as they thought, but it was a very frustrating experience. I used to think about how vulnerable, how desperate, how frightened they were—there but for the grace of God go I.

I was working as a nurse. In 1960, I went to a Presbyterian-Episcopal hospital as a clinical instructor in the School of Nursing, and then, in 1965, to a Catholic hospital primarily as a nurse in labor and delivery. I married in '59, had a baby in '60, and another one in '63. I was a Supermom.

Abortion was not discussed then. I went through nursing school in the fifties, and it was not discussed; neither was contraception. In the hospitals, they were doing abortions safely, but under the guise of something else. It was not uncommon to work in the operating room and have doctors doing "D&Cs," when you knew darn well they were doing early abortions.

I saw the privileged who could pay for it, who were educated and determined enough to make the system work for them, getting abortions. The women I saw in the hospital beds, postabortion, were the ones who couldn't do that. Women came in on the GYN wards with all sorts of conditions and you suspected—even though they would maybe never admit it—that there had been an illegal abortion. There were a lot of kidney problems, bladder problems, and infections from incomplete abortions, where fragments of tissue were left inside. Many women died from peritonitis, an infection in the abdomen, and septicemia, an infection in the bloodstream.

Absolutely, all the time, women were pressured to give the names of the abortionists, but it was the best-kept secret in the world. There was a bond there. The women would either die or go home without telling. In those days, the authorities reported an abortion just like it was a major crime—you see, it was illegal then to advise, induce, or perform an abortion in Missouri. Usually, whoever was on duty in the emergency room—a nurse, a doctor, somebody, there was not much of a protocol—would call the police. Then, they would come and interrogate the woman.

It was common for some doctors to support women who had to resort to illegal abortions, though they wouldn't *do* the abortions themselves. I remember this midwife in St. Louis who did abortions. The local doctors got her her equipment, backed her up, sent their patients to her, and followed their patients, treating them if there were complications and putting them in the hospital. Even then, the medical community didn't want to confront the issue.

I was on the suicide hotline for probably a year and a half when a handful of us in Missouri decided we wanted to deal with the abortion issue directly. So we began to do research about where the resources were, and out of that grew the Clergy Consultation Service of Missouri. We were part of a national network that was begun in the late sixties by Howard Moody and Arlene Carmen from Judson Memorial Church in Manhattan; they were the original founders of the New York and the National Clergy Consultation Service on Abortion.

There were five of us—Gwyn Harvey, the psychologist who was the director of the Suicide Prevention Hotline; myself, because I represented the medical piece; Frank Susman, the attorney who argued the *Webster* case for Reproductive Health Services, who goes way back with all of us; a Methodist minister; and a woman who was involved with the campus ministry program at the University of Missouri in Columbia and married to an Episcopalian priest.

The clergy agreed to participate because they knew that the illegal abortion rate was high. Women were dying, and their fertility was being jeopardized. There was a real commitment from Episcopal, Unitarian and Methodist ministers from around the state, from Reform and some Conservative rabbis and even from a few Catholic priests who would quietly see women. Most of the Catholic priests were Jesuits, and many ended up leaving the church.

The clergy had a cloak of confidentiality around them, which meant that they did not have to divulge the names of anyone they counseled. So we started out using just clergy as counselors, but very quickly moved into using nonclergy. We got churches to give us space, and we would send women and their families on an appointment basis to different churches around the city and then around the state. Volunteer counselors would go to the different churches for blocks of three or four hours and see these women. We helped the women through the crisis and had a referral network to send them for abortions as well as for ongoing counseling, if they needed something beyond the crisis intervention.

We had some crazy scares. I remember one night, when I was having dinner at the hospital where I worked, I got a page. My husband and my kids had come out to eat dinner with me, which they usually did. The page was from my mother-in-law, whose name, of course, was the same as mine. She said, "I just got a call from the sheriff's office in Clayton," which was the county seat. "They have some papers to serve you."

Frank Susman had always said, "Keep a dime in your shoe. If you're arrested or anything happens, call me before you open your mouth." I picked up the phone and put my dime in, but I couldn't find his number. So I called Gwyn Harvey, and she called an attorney she knew. He said, "Tell Judy to get out of the county, and we'll run a check to see if there's a warrant out for her arrest."

So here we are at the hospital. We have the two little kids, and we have another son who's at work—the first foster child we took in as a teenager. We called him and said, "Don't go home; go to somebody else's house." We took the little boys to my brother's and said, "Don't ask questions. We'll call you tomorrow."

Then my husband and I went by our house, dropped off my husband's truck, and spent the night at Gwyn's, trying to figure out who had turned us in. Remember, there was no developed anti-abortion movement then. Frank had already gone to talk with the prosecuting attorney in the county to tell him what we were doing, and he'd been looking the other way. But we were functioning illegally, and if anybody wanted to press charges, they could have.

We finally found Frank, ran a check, and there was no warrant out for my arrest. I was scheduled to go to work at four o'clock the next afternoon, so we went home. I'm in the shower, my husband is there, and the phone rings. He answered. He was doing a lot of the phone stuff in those days; he was very supportive and very involved. He came in and said, "That was the sheriff's office." I said, "Oh my God." He said—and he smiled, and I knew—"Somebody there wants your *services*. Their girlfriend's daughter is pregnant."

You can see, on one hand, our paranoia, and on the other hand—though abortion was illegal—that even people in the county sheriff's office were calling for help. I mean, an unwanted pregnancy can happen to anybody, anytime.

I'm a case in point. In 1969, I had a diaphragm failure and became pregnant. We had two children by then and one foster child. My husband and I didn't want to have any more babies. For one thing, we had an AO blood incompatibility. In those days, it could have been a fatal condition for the baby; if left untended, the baby would have been either severely brain damaged or died.

My first and second babies had to have all of their blood replaced by transfusions. The doctors were afraid that if I had any further pregnancies, they would have to deliberately induce me earlier and earlier because the closer you get to term, the more risk there is to the fetus. That gets you into the prematurity factor: Size is not the only thing that generates good health for newborns; there's also lung maturity, which premature babies, regardless of size, can lack.

My husband and I made the decision to terminate the pregnancy. We thought we had a lot of responsibility to our children already born and to ourselves. We also took into account the risk of the medical condition. I believe that every one of us secretly wants a perfect child. Some people say, "The greatest thing that happened to us was having a Down syndrome child." I laud those people, I support those people, but don't tell me that it was the best thing that ever happened—to them or to that child. Saying that is the way we deal with things, the way we cope. It's a very difficult situation to have a handicapped child. Yes, lots and lots of families rise to the occasion. Lots and lots of other families choose not to continue the pregnancy.

I felt pretty stupid about being pregnant, but also grateful that I knew where to go. I went to a medical corpsman, an army guy, a great guy, who had been in the Korean or the Second World War. I had a D&C, awake without an anesthetic. It hurt like hell. It felt like terrible cramping—intense, just intense. I was not frightened, but remember, I knew how to breathe, I had taught Lamaze, I could relax with it, and it still hurt like hell. So you can imagine what it was like for those kids who didn't know what was going to happen to them. The more they resisted, the worse the pain was.

Did I think about the abortion afterwards? Absolutely. To this day, I think, Oh, if I had continued that pregnancy, I would have a twenty-two-year-old now. Do I regret it? No. Unbeknownst to me, I would adopt two more children years later, adolescents who we had custody of until they were twenty-one. I love adolescence; it's my favorite time. Adopting those children at that point in my life was my way of filling a void, which had nothing to do with the abortion, and was also a healthy, positive thing to do.

It was at the Catholic hospital that I found out I was pregnant. In fact, I worked there for at least a year and a half while I was with Clergy Consultation. The hospital didn't know about my involvement, and I had to be very careful.

In late '69 or early '70, we decided to go public with the whole story about Clergy Consultation. There had been efforts in the legislature to remove the abortion law, and we felt it was time.

When I went public on television as coordinator of the service, I was prepared to lose my job at the Catholic hospital. I had been getting good reviews, but all of a sudden they told me that I must not be happy in my job because I was working with women who were choosing to terminate their pregnancies, but also helping women who were coming to the hospital to have babies. It was never a conflict for me. As a professional, I was there to help women implement a choice, not make a judgment. But it was a conflict for the hospital, so I quit. After that, I went with Clergy Consultation full-time, doing training and supervision at our five centers around the state and making a whole two thousand dollars a year.

The work was new and challenging, and resources were opening up all the time. Through the late sixties and into the early seventies, we had been referring women to Mexico, where they would get off the airplane with a white ribbon on their lapels so they could be easily identified. In 1967, Colorado and California liberalized their laws to permit abortions in some circumstances, and in 1970, New York actually repealed its anti-abortion law and the procedure became legal. Around that time, Washington, D.C., and New Mexico opened up, too.

We were referring about thirty to forty patients a week just from Saint Louis, population probably a million then. The bulk of the women needed first-trimester abortions, so they were candidates for New York, but we also took them to the other states. We took them to the Manhattan clinic started by Dr. Hale Harvey, who I consider the father of ambulatory abortion services; the Preterm Clinic in Washington, D.C.; a clinic in Westchester, New York; and a hospital in Los Angeles where we had a doctor who did second-trimester abortions.

We were getting women from all over the state of Missouri, including way up in the rural areas. A lot of them were married women, about 30 percent. We would spend more time getting them ready to go to an airport, fly on an airplane, and go to New

York City than preparing them for the procedure. They were terrified . . . terrified.

I flew back and forth to New York once a month, out of the agency money that we raised, to be with the women going for the abortions, to monitor the facilities, to follow them back, and to try to work out situations where clinics would take poor women—if we could get the air fare—and do one out of ten abortions for free.

I did in-service on TWA up the kazoo. After the stewardesses had finished with food service, they'd be in the back of the plane chatting, and I'd spend time with them. I'd say, "Do you know you have nine women on this plane who had abortions in the last four hours? What would you do if one of them hemorrhaged?" They'd be shocked to know that so many women in that situation were on the plane, and realized they were not prepared. If anything happened, they would have had to tell the pilot to land the plane.

Remember, until then, abortion had been an in-hospital, general anesthesia procedure. Now, we were doing the procedure in an ambulatory setting, and the women were getting up off the table, spending an hour or two in the recovery room, and then being taken to the airport and flown home. There was the risk of hemorrhage, though we know now that risk is much lower than we thought in those days. Often, bleeding occurs not because it's a sloppy job but because the uterus just doesn't contract. And some of the women were second-trimester patients, where the risk of bleeding could be higher. So I taught the stewardesses fundal massage to the uterus, which helps make the uterus—a muscle—contract. I told them about getting the patient prone and how to use ice.

I tried to get TWA to incorporate that kind of training into the flight attendant program, because everybody was schlepping a lot of women who had just had abortions. We tried to get group

air rates so we could cut the costs. But the airlines were uncoop-
erative.

Clergy Consultation in Missouri helped thousands of people
and stayed in business from 1967 until 1973, when *Roe* v. *Wade*
legalized abortion throughout the nation. *Roe* was absolutely a
shock to everybody. We knew that the case had been heard. We
knew that Sarah Weddington had argued. But I, for one, was
not very well connected to the political piece in those days, and
just never expected it to happen.

I was sitting at my desk at our Clergy Consultation office in
St. Louis, and I got a call—I think from Harry Levin, founder
of the Preterm Clinic group—at about 9:20 A.M. I was smart
enough to know we were making a quantum leap, as I found
myself getting up out of my chair. It was just unbelievable. You
didn't know what to do. One minute it's illegal and we have this
whole system in place, and the next minute it's legal and we've
got all these rights.

The elation over *Roe* v. *Wade* got channeled into a spirit of
"Let's move, let's do it, let's be the first, let's get out there," and
boy, it was fast. I called an emergency board meeting and a press
conference. At one board meeting, we had decided that, when
abortion became legal, we would open a clinic to do abortions,
so I announced that we would begin on March 8. I knew we
wouldn't make that date, but I wanted to hook the press because
that was the best way to let women all over the state know that
abortion was now legal.

On May 22, we did open the first abortion outpatient clinic
in the state of Missouri and in the Midwest. We could have
opened a month earlier than that, but our first doctor refused
to do any procedures until the Eighth Circuit Court, the federal
court in Kansas City, had actually said that the existing law in
Missouri was no more.

We offered counseling, abortion, and contraceptive education.

Finally, every woman who needed an abortion wouldn't have to get on an airplane. Those who had to travel would be traveling, at most, from three hundred miles across the state instead of two or three thousand miles across the country. Finally, we'd only have to take care of women and their families. Oh, gosh, we were excited. We expected things to get easier. . . . We were so naive.

The day we opened Reproductive Health Services, we had pickets, but it was peaceful, sidewalk picketing. We had been very visible media-wise, so we knew we were going to have some hassles. Remember, we're three blocks from the St. Louis Cathedral, and St. Louis is heavily Catholic. The archdiocese formed a pro-life committee and assigned each parish a time to picket 100 North Euclid. For the first four or five years, we had pickets daily, but they stayed on the sidewalks and didn't do anything aggressive.

It was in the late seventies that we began to see militant anti-choice activists like Joe Scheidler, a right-wing Catholic from Chicago, a former Benedictine seminarian with lots of kids, who started the Pro-Life Action League and wrote *Closed: 99 Ways to Stop Abortion.* Randall Terry, founder of Operation Rescue, is one of his disciples. By 1985, we were the site for an action by a militant anti-choice group; there were about three hundred people at the clinic from some fifteen states, and I remember sixty-one arrests.

Bomb threats and death threats, which began in the early 1970s, got worse. I got death threats by mail. I got them in the middle of the night. People called on the phone and said, "You dirty baby killer. You're going to die. I'd be careful getting in my car tomorrow morning if I were you." Scared the shit out of me. I reported it all to ATF [the U.S. Department of Alcohol, Tobacco, and Firearms]. They did a lot of in-services with us. They would tell us to move around with caution, not to take the same route home every night.

In June of 1986, after we had opened a second clinic site in western St. Louis County, we were firebombed. It was about 12:20 at night when I got the call. I'd been to the symphony, and I was sitting out on my back porch with a friend when the phone rang. The call was from the police. I had a key, and they needed someone to come out there because, they said, "West County's on fire."

I went in and rousted my youngest son, who is kind of my soul child and also the one who'd been working at the clinic at the time, and his friend who was staying here. The building is in a fairly well populated area, but it sits kind of low. As we drove out there, I could see the flames in the sky. It was just awful. It was my worst nightmare come true.

The fire damaged the reception area, the waiting room—$100,000 worth. The whole building would have gone up if there hadn't been a skylight right above where they threw the cans of gasoline. The skylight blew out from the intensity, allowing everything to escape. There were two other doctors who did abortions in that building. There's no question they were trying to get rid of the whole thing.

Things began to sour from a political standpoint, too, by the late seventies. We already had no Medicaid funding. We had it until the federal Hyde Amendment took effect in 1977, prohibiting Medicaid payment for poor women's abortions except if the woman's life was in danger; Missouri fell right after that. From the mid-seventies on, the Missouri legislature had been very active in promulgating legislation that was basically unconstitutional, that did not fit within the framework of *Roe.* Pro-choice organizations, including Reproductive Health Services, began to sue the state of Missouri for legislation that had been passed, requiring things like parental consent and spousal consent. *Webster* v. *Reproductive Health Services* was the fifth case out of the state of Missouri to reach the Supreme Court. But it was the first case where there was a new court, and it had national implications; everybody was watching.

Since *Webster*—which upheld Missouri's law forbidding public employees and pubic facilities from doing abortions, as well as requiring viability tests on all pregnant women after twenty weeks—we've found women from outside the metropolitan areas being forced to carry pregnancies to term because they can't locate hospitals or doctors to do their abortions. And you can see *Webster*'s impact beyond Missouri every time you pick up the newspaper—another state's going to limit abortion, another state's going to develop a copycat law to *Webster*.

But my real concern about the impact of *Webster* is a scenario as follows: The decision says, You cannot do abortions in publicly funded hospitals. What is a publicly funded hospital? A private hospital that got federal funds to build? That gets Medicaid funds? There isn't a private institution that doesn't get some kind of federal money for something. Since *Webster*, some hospitals in Missouri are taking a very conservative interpretation and, even though they are not publicly funded institutions, choosing not to provide abortions. *Webster* just gives them one more excuse.

Today, the bulk of the American people don't want abortion to be illegal, but they don't want to talk about it either. There's a lot of ambivalence. We did a survey of Missourians; what it said was that they believed abortion should be legal, but also that it should be regulated.

Some of that ambivalence has surfaced as a result of our allowing the other side to frame the debate, and they framed it by focusing on the fetus, which doesn't allow us to deal with any of the complexities of this issue. Yes, probably we focused on the woman as opposed to the fetus, but I don't think that was inappropriate at that time. We were emerging; we needed to talk about women's rights. But I'll tell you, women's rights don't sell in Peoria today. Women don't sell as well as babies sell, quite frankly.

We may have dropped the ball in the last five years, when we should have been making a little bit more of a move toward some compromise language. There are still pro-choice people, for example, who disagree with *Roe* and feel that abortion should be subject to no governmental regulation through all nine months of pregnancy. I think they're crazy. If that were to be what we insisted on, we'd lose the whole shooting match.

I think one of our compromise points has to do with viability, which is currently established at approximately twenty-four weeks. To me, life's a continuum. A fetus is biological life, but then, in itself, so is a cell. The issue has to do with when the fetus has survivability, capability, outside the womb, and I mean survivability with a quality of life. Only one half of one percent of all abortions are done after twenty weeks, and it seems to me, from a pragmatic, political standpoint, that we can set the cutoff for abortions at twenty-two weeks, with provisions for emergency cases, and try to educate and help those women who delay abortions, who tend to be poor women and minors. That's what we've done at Reproductive Health Services.

I don't think that anything that happened, even pre-'73, was as frightening as now. I was naive and young and learning in the sixties when abortion was illegal. I had nothing to compare it to. Now I have a comparison. To lose safe and legal abortion would mean incredible devastation for families, women, and children. It would mean reducing women to childbearing vessels again. It would mean turning our backs on the technology we have and refusing to take the responsibility to use it. And the other thing it would say to me is that, twenty years after *Roe*, we still don't value women as independent human beings. By taking away abortion, the real message is: You don't have a right to decide.

Norma McCorvey

(alias Jane Roe)

After keeping her identity a secret for nearly a decade, Norma McCorvey came out as the real *Jane Roe*, named plaintiff in the landmark Supreme Court case that in 1973 legalized abortion in the United States. Recent stepped-up threats to legal abortion and an attempt on her life have led her to become an even more vocal pro-choice voice.

Forty-five-year-old McCorvey, who had three children, was born in Louisiana. Today, she makes her home in Texas.

When I got pregnant with the *Roe* baby, I was in Georgia working in a carnival. I went back to Dallas, Texas, where I'd lived the better part of my life. I was roughly twenty, twenty-one then, and it was 1969. I decided I couldn't bring another child into the world.

That was my third pregnancy. When I got pregnant the first time, I was married. I got married when I was sixteen, so I was about seventeen and a half when I had my first child. She was born in 1965. I didn't want to have a baby right off the bat, but I wanted to have a child—I wanted to have a family.

I was a very good mother when I had my daughter, the first one, but after my marriage broke up, my mother took her away from me. She was upset that I was working in a gay bar. I was working as a waitress. Sometimes I'd work two shifts and wouldn't come home until four or five in the evening. She took care of Missy during the day. She had child welfare follow me around—they came to my job.

I had my second child, another daughter, in 1967. The man I was involved with wanted to get married, to put a white picket fence in the front yard, but I didn't. I didn't know which direction I was really going to go in then, and I think that had a lot to do with my depression. I gave my second child to the father and promised I would never, ever bother them again, and I haven't. I know she's in good hands.

I never heard about birth control until I had my second child. I grew up without any discussion of sex, without any talk about birth control. My mother was Catholic, my father was a Jehovah's Witness, and the word "sex" wasn't mentioned in my house.

At the time of my second pregnancy, I wasn't using birth control because I didn't know where to get it, and I was too ashamed to ask for it—that's all it boiled down to. Condoms were called rubbers when I was growing up. Girls didn't buy them—it wasn't thought of, at least on my part. A diaphragm would have meant going to a doctor, right? See, if I was to ask for birth control or anything like that, then everybody would know what I was doing, that I wasn't married and I was having sex. But I constantly worried that I was pregnant. I used to buy that Massengil douche powder and use that—we were all so naive.

When I got pregnant with the *Roe* baby, I knew I couldn't take care of a child. I wasn't working at the time. I lived with my dad. I wasn't really destitute—I had food to eat and a roof over my head—but I didn't have any jingle in my pocket, and I really didn't have a whole lot of ambition.

I went to an abortion clinic, an illegal abortion clinic, in Dallas. Actually, I believe it was a dentistry clinic, and they were using the back portion of it to do abortions. I got real bad vibes when I walked up to it, but then I was scared as hell, too. The place had been busted. It was abandoned. There was still some stuff there, but no people. It was very eerie. So, I had no choice at all. I stood there maybe for fifteen minutes or so, and I cried. I don't know why—just being scared, just wanting something to happen that I knew would never happen.

My doctor recommended that I go see this attorney, Henry McClusky, Jr., about adoption, though I really wanted an abortion. When I met Henry—and it was love at first sight—I was almost two and a half months pregnant, but I hadn't given up yet on abortion.

I met Sarah Weddington and Linda Coffee, who argued *Roe*, through Henry. He told me that he knew these two young law students who might be able to help me, and asked, would I like to be a plaintiff? I said, "What's a plaintiff?"

So Sarah and I and Linda met and talked. They didn't really lead me to think they could actually get me an abortion; I was just *hoping* so much. I did say I was raped. See, I had talked to a lot of women, and they said that the best way to get an abortion was to tell that I had been raped. The worse the crime, the better the chance of getting an abortion, so I concocted this whole story out of my imagination—out of desperation, really.

Of course, I didn't understand about the court system and how it worked. I do a little now. We had to sue the district attorney first or something like that, then we had to file in federal court, and then, I lost track after the second or third court.

I remember waiting. You'd go around all day in the house.

You'd do this and you'd do that; you'd try to keep yourself occupied. You'd go out and look for a job. You'd get up and starch and iron your best waitress uniform. You'd spend practically the last dime you had in getting wherever you needed to go for an interview, and then nobody wanted to take you on just because you were pregnant.

I agreed to be the plaintiff because I was pissed. I thought, Well, this is a hell of a world we're in. We're women, and we get second-class jobs; we get second-class pay; it's always second-class this, second-class that. I thought, That's not fair. I just decided that if I stayed with Sarah and Linda, I might have at least a fifty-fifty chance . . . maybe, maybe, if I stuck with these two people, they could really do it. And sure enough, they did, but not for me, no.

By the time you're well into your fifth month, you're beginning to realize, I'm going to have to have this baby. Once I realized that I could not have a legal, therapeutic abortion, I accepted the fact that the child would be put in a very good home. Henry found the home. He said, "They're not extremely rich, but they want a baby." So you finally accept it, and you deal with it. I know I may make it sound easy, but it wasn't.

After I gave birth, they took the baby away from me, and then they brought the baby to me in my room when they had all the other babies out. Once they realized that they had screwed up, they came in and yanked the baby out of my arms. I got hysterical. I nearly took the nurse out. Had she not been carrying my baby, I would have taken her out right there. It was very devastating.

They moved me to a private room and sedated me. I woke up from time to time, real groggy and sick to my stomach. I went into a very deep depression.

After that, I went back to my dad's. I'd sleep all day and all night, sometimes forty-eight, seventy-two hours, just sleep, sleep, sleep. Henry called me a couple times and said, "I just want to let you know that everything's okay." When he called, I think, the third time, I was in a real bad space. I told him, "I don't want you to call me no more . . . I don't want to know."

I just wanted to check out . . . I figured it wasn't my time to be here. I tried to commit suicide after I had the baby. I have scars on my arms from cutting my wrists. My dad found me. I got the courage to go on when I got a job at a hospital; I just decided I wasn't going to be so rough on myself anymore. What's done is done; it can't be undone. After I had the *Roe* baby, I finally straightened out everything that was wrong and just kept on living.

About the *Roe* baby, the only thing I can actually say is that I have signed a document of confidentiality, which means that I find out things about her, but I can't talk about it. I signed that document last June. Before that, I didn't know anything about her. I know she's fine now—she's fine, and that's enough.

Roe v. *Wade* really wasn't very important to me at first, I have to say that honestly. I really felt like I had been cheated because the decision didn't help me. But then, when I began to fully understand what the decision meant, I was very proud to be part of that, and I'm still proud.

I did my first interview in 1980 as Norma McCorvey, the real Jane Roe. It took something like four hours for maybe seven seconds of air time. I was really ready to come out at that point, but I still hadn't grasped the whole issue—not to insinuate that I'm an expert on abortion now, because I'm not.

I never knew I'd come out publicly. When I was working down in Austin about ten years ago, around a lot of political people, they started saying, "You could do this . . . you could do that . . . you should understand who you are . . . what you've done for women." I'd say, "I know what I've done." But then I got to thinking one night, Dummy. You helped to change the course of history for all the women in America. I decided to break my anonymity.

I started coming out as Jane Roe in 1980, then I'd go back and hide in my house and come out on the next anniversary of the decision. I was always very timid, very shy. Then, beginning in 1989, I came out much stronger. What changed? They shot at me.

It was April 4, 1989, and I was in Dallas. We were fixing to go to the pro-choice march on Washington. At 4:10 A.M., somebody drove by and shot the back windshield of my car out. Then, they shot my damn house up. They shot right into the living room—shattered the glass of a new storm door and two living room windows. I woke out of a dead sleep. I had no idea what was going on. It was very loud . . . it was a ten-gauge shotgun blast. If I had been sleeping on the couch, they would have been digging the bullets out of my skull.

When I came down into the living room, they were fixing to fire the last shot into the storm door. My roommate said, "Bite the carpet!" Man, I bit the carpet. The last shot went just over my head.

I called the police. When they first walked in, they said, "Have either one of you girls recently broke up with anyone?" They didn't know who I was . . . I kept my identity pretty concealed. I remember the cop said, "Apparently, one or both of you-all have an enemy." And I said, "Gee, I wonder what gave you that idea?" That's when I completely broke down.

My roommate told the police who I was. The cop turned around and had this look on his face. Then he said he was going out to his car to make a radio call. I said, "Shit, I'm calling the FBI," and I did. That's actually when I first started feeling the impact. I walked outside, looked back in the house, and thought, Hot damn, girl. You nearly bought the farm. They'd nearly killed me.

We had to replace the windows; the insurance picked up that tab. They damaged the couch, but I didn't have any renter's insurance to cover it. They damn near hit my stereo, and I had just made the last payment on it. I had to replace the back windshield of my car; my insurance had just expired, and it cost quite a bit of money. I was a bond runner at the time, working nights, making five dollars an hour.

It was like living in prison in that house after that, because we had twenty-four-hour security. A real good friend of mine in New York, the company she works for, paid for that. That happened in April, and I moved in June to California. I keep everything secret . . . my address, my phone number. I do it out of habit.

I don't know how it feels to be a threat to people. I never considered myself a threat, up until they shot up the house. I had gotten some hate mail. I'd found baby clothes thrown in my front yard. I'd had a few notes here and there, never threatening my life, just like, "Baby Killer," "Murderess," you know.

The shooting made me determined to be more public. It would have been easy to take the safe way out, to hide, but I'm not a person who takes the easy way out. I've never been in any kind of safe situation in my life.

Roe v. *Wade* is most definitely more a part of my life now. Down in Sonoma County, they've named an organization after me. It's called ROE—Reproductive Options for Everyone.

Dimensions

of

Legal

Abortion

B y l l y e   A v e r y

Byllye Avery has devoted more than twenty years of her life to improv-
ing the health of American women, particularly black women. She
helped to found the first abortion clinic in Gainesville, Florida, and one
of the state's first freestanding birthing centers. In 1981, she established
the National Black Women's Health Project, a unique self-help advocacy organization that has over 130 groups in twenty-two states and
six foreign countries. Avery's commitment and vision were rewarded in
1988 with a so-called Genius Award from the John D. and Catherine
T. MacArthur Foundation, a five-year, no-strings-attached fellowship.

Widowed in 1970 at the age of thirty-three, Avery is the mother of two
grown children. She makes her home in Boston.

Once abortion became legal in
1973, four of us would drive women from Gainesville, Florida,
to Jacksonville—an hour and a half away—where there was a
Saturday abortion clinic. I worked on the Children's Mental
Health Unit at Shands Teaching Hospital as head teacher; two
of the other women worked on the unit and one was a nurse.
We ended up using our Saturdays to transport women, but it
didn't take us very long to get to the point where we realized
this couldn't go on. We decided to open a clinic in Gainesville.
We knew that the local medical society would not approve—

147

nobody but doctors opened up clinics then—but there were no regulations saying we couldn't set a clinic up, so we took advantage of a void.

What we did was find an old building that had been used by the Health Department. Lucky for us, it was owned by a woman who taught at the University of Florida, so we felt pretty secure in there. The first thing we did was renovate the building and make it an absolutely wonderful space. We painted the walls in nice colors. The furniture in the living room was all denim. We put plants in all the rooms, even the bathrooms, and hung lots of wonderful posters. In the recovery room, we had one couch and several recliners because we felt that the women did not necessarily need to be laid out in beds. It was very beautifully done. You've got to understand what a revolutionary thing this was in 1974—abortion clinics were the forerunners of the free-standing treatment centers that have been set up throughout the United States.

To finance the clinic, each of us borrowed from the credit union to the max. Then we opened up accounts and charged the furniture, which came out of the Sears catalog. Our two vacuum aspirators [standard equipment to perform an abortion from seven to thirteen weeks] came from Clergy Consultation—I think, in New York—because they were shutting down their centers. They cost two thousand dollars apiece, which back in '74 was a lot of money.

When we took over the building, it had this old, horrible-looking tile floor. The nurse who was working with us said, "We have to cover up this floor." But we'd spent so much money on equipment, supplies, and furniture that we didn't know how we could come up with another two thousand dollars for what we wanted, which was a shag rug. She told us she was going to ask her mother-in-law to lend us the money, then told us her mother-in-law said we could have it.

What we didn't know was that, actually, she had ordered the

rug and charged it to us. When we found out, we were so upset with her, but the carpet is what made the place. We had a beautiful blue shag rug that went though the whole clinic, even the exam rooms. That's what everybody who came there talked about—shag carpets were the rage. It was also that we had the gall to say, "We don't have to have these horrible tile floors just because this is a health-care facility." It helped women to know that abortions didn't have to be bloody and butchery. Certainly, you wouldn't put that kind of a rug on the floor if it was going to be ruined.

The Gainesville Women's Health Center opened up in May of 1974 with a big spread in the *Gainesville Sun.* You had to have a medical director who would sign your protocols and provide medical backup and supervision; we went to Jacksonville and got a physician there to be our medical director. This doctor was a champion for the cause and willing to take the risk of being ostracized by other physicians. The abortions were actually done by residents from a hospital in Jacksonville on their days off. If there were any emergencies, then Shands Teaching Hospital had to provide care, but we couldn't make any official arrangement with the hospital staff.

The three women I helped to open the clinic with in Gainesville were white, and while we were close friends, many times I was the only black woman in the area doing this kind of work. I used to sometimes question: What am I doing here? Why am I working on abortion? It would be years before I got those answers, which came when I started the National Black Women's Health Project and understood how all of my previous experiences came into play.

A lot of black families came to the Gainesville Women's Center to get abortions. Previously, I had thought that not many black women got abortions, but what was really happening was that we didn't have a way to talk about it. Folks were participating in a conspiracy of silence.

When I was growing up in DeLand, Florida, the way people talked about abortion was to say, "So-and-so threw away her baby," which gave a graphic picture of abortion as an act of irresponsibility rather than one of responsibility, which is what I think it is. Folks didn't talk about sex. My mother told me, "If you get pregnant, I'll kill you. . . . You're going to college." I went to Talladega College and had an absolutely wonderful time. That's where I met my husband, and that's where my daughter just graduated from.

I remember when I was in college one of my friends got pregnant. She went somewhere and came back with these big black pills. We didn't know what they were. They didn't make her abort, but she certainly tried. You heard all kinds of stories about folks drinking turpentine, kerosene, doing almost anything to keep from being pregnant. There was that fear that pregnancy could get you at any time. If your period was a few days late, if you threw up—even if you hadn't been sexually active—you started thinking, Maybe I'm pregnant. We were functioning with a lot of ignorance and fear.

I don't see how you could have grown up then not thinking that abortion was a bad thing. What I came to realize is that life is very complicated, and abortion is often a very painful and hard decision.

I had a legal abortion in 1973. My head had changed around before that on the subject of abortion. In the early seventies, there was the whole upsurge of feminism. Our feelings about abortion were influenced by a new consciousness about rape, incest, the role sexism plays in the development of our sexuality, and a commitment to claiming our bodies.

I wasn't married at the time I got my abortion. It was after my husband died. He had had a massive heart attack at thirty-three, and I was left with these two little kids. They were young, and I certainly wasn't about to have another baby. Trying to raise them alone was as much as I could deal with.

When I found out I was pregnant, I already knew what I would decide. Most women know whether or not it is a good time for them to be having children. If you're having a hard time yourself, the answer's pretty obvious.

I was having a hard time. I had a lot going for me—a master's degree and a good job as head teacher at Shands—but emotionally, it was very hard. I was not really a single parent; I was a double parent. I had nobody to bounce anything off of. Every decision affecting the lives of two more individuals rested with me—getting them to their dental appointments, going to all the football games, talking to the teacher, getting their homework done, doing the laundry, keeping the food on the table, you know what I'm saying?

I wasn't using any birth control the time I got pregnant. I had been using the diaphragm pretty religiously, but this was just one of those times. I was away. I knew I was going to be with another friend and her kids, and I was going to have my kids. You think: What are the chances of my getting loose from all this? So you don't bother bringing anything . . . you're unprepared. Then, you meet somebody, and *Bam!* That's the time something happens.

But, remember, from the time a girl gets her period—mine started at eleven—all the way up to when she's menopausal, you're talking about some forty, fifty years of twelve times a year that you can get pregnant. If you multiply twelve months times forty years, what is that, about five hundred months? The law of averages says you're going to mess up *sometime* no matter how faithful you are. What I learned from that experience is that women should carry their birth control with them all the time . . . that's my advice.

I was nervous about the abortion. If you've got to go and have surgery, you're scared. The nurse said to me, "People have all kinds of reactions to abortion. Some cry . . . they're real upset when it's over." Well, when mine was over, I was hysterical with laughter. I just couldn't stop laughing. I think it was anxiety. You know how you yawn when you're anxious? That was the form of relief for me . . . it was relief.

I never wondered what was aborted . . . nothing like that. I personally believe that abortion is the taking of a *potential* life; that potential life does not become an actual life until it is born and breathing on its own. Women know full well what they're doing—a potential life is not as important as an actual life, and sometimes women have to make that choice.

The no-choice people are only concerned about potential life, and I think the reasoning behind their whole movement is based a lot on racism. Black infant mortality is worse in this country than it is in many Third World countries. Look at all the homeless people we've got on the street. What do you think is going to happen if abortion becomes illegal and another million and a half people are born? If the no-choice people were not racist, they would be looking at black infant mortality, at homelessness, at the conditions of oppressed people in this country, but there's never any mention of that.

Racism is also manifest in that movement in that they're talking about *white* babies, not black. There are so many white people who want to have babies but can't because of infertility due to sexually transmitted diseases, delayed pregnancy, and problems caused by poorly developed birth control technology like the IUD. But there ain't enough white babies around to adopt because the white girls are opting to either keep their babies or have abortions. So the anti-choice movement is trying to cut down on those white girls' abortions. It doesn't give a damn about black women and black babies. It just wants abortion stopped. Women of color and black women happen to be caught in the cross fire.

While I might set some limits on abortion for myself personally, I don't think that should be confused with the fact that choice needs to be available to all women. We can't go around making laws based on what people personally want or don't want to do. I agree with the *Roe* framework, which permits second-trimester abortions and even third-trimester abortions in those rare circumstances when the woman's health or life is in danger. You see, women can die trying to have an illegal second-trimester abortion just as easily as they can trying to have an illegal first-trimester one.

When people talk about pro-choice folks needing to compromise more, I say, What's the exchange? And, compromise for what? I don't think it will work to set the cutoff for abortions even earlier than the point of viability because the anti-choice people think viability starts at the moment of conception. There isn't much difference for them between twenty-four weeks and two days. I don't think a compromise like that will accomplish anything, except maybe to deprive a woman who needs a legal abortion from getting one.

As far as this thinking in terms of compromise is concerned, poor women have been the victims. There is no federal funding for poor women's abortions. Because of that, and because of the severe shortage of abortion providers, poor women are the ones who end up having abortions later in their pregnancies, or who can't get abortions at all and must raise a child they cannot afford. Their options are being more and more reduced.

In 1978, we opened Birthplace, one of the first freestanding birthing centers in Florida. At the local hospital, doctors had control of birth and gave you drugs. Women came to us because they wanted natural childbirth.

That was when I began to develop a clear understanding of not only how important it was for women to have access to abortion, but how important it was to give women whatever they needed to have a healthy baby, which involved being sure that the woman first was healthy herself. I started realizing that, no wonder infant mortality was twice as high among blacks as whites—whites were twice as healthy. Even today, white women don't have as much lupus, high blood pressure, diabetes, cardio-vascular disease. So I broadened my issues from abortion to birthing to reproductive health to black women's health in general, and in 1981 founded the National Black Women's Health Project.

Women who belong to the NBWHP are trying to understand what's going on with abortion today—what the laws are—and learning to feel comfortable, a lot of them for the first time, talking about their abortions and reproductive health. To have more black women involved in pro-choice work, you've got to first give us black women a chance to come together ourselves to talk about these issues.

The NBWHP's self-help groups focus on empowerment. When you're choosing how you want to be in the world, being able to choose abortion is just as much a part of that as being able to choose if, where, when, and how you will have a baby. It's all intertwined. For us, as African-American women who came up through slavery and were forced to breed, we can't ever give away the opportunity to make those decisions for ourselves.

R a y n a   R a p p

Rayna Rapp is a professor in and chair of the anthropology department at the New School for Social Research in New York City. Her current research, which grows out of the experience she describes in the essay that follows (originally published in *Test Tube Women: What Future For Motherhood?* edited by Rita Arditti, Unwin Hyman, 1984, and in a shorter version in the April 1984 issue of *Ms.* magazine), focuses on how women of different classes, races, ethnic and religious backgrounds deal with the experience and consequences of amniocentesis. Rapp has been active in the reproductive rights movement and in the movement for women's studies for over twenty years.

Forty-six years old and recently remarried, Rapp has an eight-year-old daughter and an infant son.

Mike called the fetus XYLO, XY for its unknown sex, LO for the love we were pouring into it. Day by day we fantasized about who this growing cluster of cells might become. Day by day, we followed the growth process in the myriad books that surround modern pregnancy for the over-thirty-five baby boomlet. Both busy with engrossing work and political commitments, we welcomed this potential child with excitement, fantasy, and the rationality of scientific knowledge. As a Women's Movement activist, I had decided opinions about treating pregnancy as a normal, not a diseased condition, and we were fortunate to find a health-care team—obstetrician, mid-wives, genetic counselor—who shared that view.

The early months of the pregnancy passed in a blur of exhaustion and nausea. Preoccupied with my own feelings, I lived in a perpetual underwater, slow-motion version of my prior life. As one friend put it, I was already operating on fetal time, tied to an unfamiliar regimen of enforced naps, loss of energy, and rigid eating. Knowing the research on nutrition, on hormones, and on miscarriage rates among older pregnant women, I did whatever I could to stay comfortable.

I was thirty-six when XYLO was conceived, and like many of my peers, I chose to have amniocentesis, a prenatal test for birth defects such as Down syndrome, Tay-Sachs disease, and sickle-cell anemia. Both Mike and I knew about prenatal diagnosis from our friends' experiences, and from reading about it. Each year, many thousands of American women choose amniocentesis to detect birth defects. The procedure is performed between the sixteenth and twentieth weeks of pregnancy. Most obstetricians, mine included, send their pregnant patients directly to the genetic division of a hospital where counseling is provided, and the laboratory technicians are specially trained. Analysis of amniotic fluid requires complex laboratory work, and can cost between five hundred dollars and two thousand dollars.

It was fear of Down syndrome that sent us to seek prenatal diagnosis of XYLO. Down syndrome produces a characteristic physical appearance—short, stocky size, large tongue, puffy upward-slanting eyes with skin folds in the inner corners—and is a major cause of mental retardation, worldwide. People with Down syndrome are quite likely to have weak cardiovascular systems, respiratory problems, and run a greater risk of developing childhood leukemia. While the majority of Down syndrome infants used to die very young, a combination of antibiotics and infant surgery enables modern medicine to keep them alive. And programs of childhood physical-mental stimulation may facili-

tate their assimilation. Some parents also opt for cosmetic surgery—an expensive and potentially risky procedure. Down syndrome is caused by an extra chromosome, at the twenty-first pair
of chromosomes, as geneticists label them. And while the diagnosis of Down spells mental retardation and physical vulnerabil-
ity, no geneticist can tell you how seriously affected your
particular fetus will be. There is no cure for Down syndrome.
A pregnant woman whose fetus is diagnosed as having the extra
chromosome can either prepare to raise a mentally retarded and
physically vulnerable child, or decide to abort it.

On the February morning Mike and I arrived at a local
medical center for genetic counseling, in my nineteenth week of
pregnancy, Nancy Z., our counselor, took a detailed pedigree (or
family tree) from each of us, to discover any rare diseases or
birth defects for which we could be tested. She then gave us an
excellent genetics lesson, explained the amniocentesis procedure and the risks, both of the test and of discovering a serious
genetic defect. One third of one percent of pregnancies miscarry
due to amniocentesis. Most women feel fine after the test, but
some (perhaps 10 percent) experience uterine cramping or con-
tractions. Overall, about 98 percent of the women who go for
amniocentesis will be told that no fetal defects or anomalies have
been found.

After counseling, we descended to the testing area, where an
all-female team of radiologist, obstetrician, nurses, and staff
assistants performed the tap. In skilled hands, and with the use
of sonogram equipment, the tap is a rapid procedure. I spent
perhaps five minutes on the table, belly attached to sonar elec-
trodes, Mike holding my feet for encouragement. The radiologist
snapped Polaroid pictures of XYLO, and we had our first "baby
album"—gray blotches of a head and spine of our baby-in-
waiting. She located the placenta, which enabled the obstetrician to successfully draw a small, clear sample of amniotic fluid
(less than one eighth of a cup). The tap felt like a crampier

version of drawing blood—not particularly painful or traumatic. We marched the fluid back to the genetic lab where it would be cultured, and went home.

The waiting period for amniocentesis results is a long one, and I was very anxious. Cells must be cultured, then analyzed, a process that takes two to four weeks. We wait, caught between the late date at which amniocentesis can be performed (usually sixteen to twenty weeks); the moment of quickening, when the woman feels the fetus move (roughly eighteen to twenty weeks); and the legal limits of abortion (very few of which are performed after twenty-four weeks in the United States). Those of my friends who have had amniocentesis report terrible fantasies, dreams, and crying fits, and I was no exception: I dreamed in lurid detail of my return to the lab, of awful damage. I woke up frantic, sobbing, to face the nagging fear that is focused in the waiting period after amniocentesis.

For the 98 percent of women whose amniotic fluid reveals no anomaly, reassurance arrives by phone, or more likely, by mail, confirming a negative test. When Nancy called me twelve days after the tap, I began to scream as soon as I recognized her voice; in her office, I knew only positive results (very negative results, from a potential parent's point of view) are reported by phone. The image of myself, alone, screaming into a white plastic telephone is indelible. Although it only took twenty minutes to locate Mike and bring him and a close friend to my side, time is suspended in my memory. I replay the call, and my screams echo for indefinite periods. We learned, after contacting our midwives and obstetrician, that a diagnosis of a male fetus with Down syndrome had been made. Our fantasies for XYLO, our five months' fetus, were completely shattered.

Mike and I had discussed what we would do if amniocentesis revealed a serious genetic condition long before the test. For us, the diagnosis of Down syndrome was reason to choose abortion. Our thinking was clear, if abstract, long before the question became reality. We were eager to have a child, and prepared to change our lives to make emotional, social, and economic resources available. But the realities of raising a child who could never grow to independence would call forth more than we could muster, unless one or both of us gave up our work, our political commitments, our social existence beyond the household. And despite a shared commitment to coparenting, we both understood that in this society, that one was likely to be the mother. When I thought about myself, I knew that in such a situation, I would transform myself to become the kind of twenty-four-hour-a-day advocate such a child would require. I'd do the best and most loving job I could, and I'd undoubtedly become an activist in support of the needs of disabled children.

But other stark realities confronted us: to keep a Down syndrome child alive through potentially lethal health problems is an act of love with weighty consequences. As we ourselves age, to whom would we leave the person XYLO would become? Neither Mike nor I have any living kin who are likely to be young enough, or close enough, to take on this burden after our deaths. In a society where the state provides virtually no decent, humane services for the mentally retarded, how could we take responsibility for the future of our dependent Down syndrome child? In good conscience, we couldn't choose to raise a child who would become a ward of the state. The health care, schools, various therapies that Down syndrome children require are inadequately available, and horrendously expensive in America; no single family should have to shoulder all the burdens that a decent health and social policy may someday extend to physically and mentally disabled people. In the meantime, while struggling for such a society, we did not choose to bring a child into this world who could never grow up to care for himself.

Most women who've opted for amniocentesis are prepared to face the question of abortion, and many of us *do* choose it, after a diagnosis of serious disability is made. Perhaps 95 percent of

Down syndrome pregnancies are terminated after test results are known. Reports on other diseases and conditions are harder to find, but in one study, the diagnosis of spina bifida led to abortion about 90 percent of the time.

In shock and grief, I learned from my obstetrician that two kinds of late second-trimester abortions were available. Most common are the "installation procedures"—saline solution or urea is injected into the uterus to kill the fetus, and drugs are sometimes used to bring on labor. The woman then goes through labor to deliver the fetus. The second kind of mid-trimester abortion, and the one I chose, is a D&E—dilation and evacuation. This procedure demands more active intervention from a doctor, who vacuums out the amniotic fluid, and then removes the fetus. The D&E requires some intense, upsetting work for the medical team, but it's over in about twenty minutes, without putting the woman through labor. Both forms of late abortion entail some physical risk, and the psychological pain is enormous. Deciding to end the life of a fetus you've wanted and carried for most of five months is no easy matter. The number of relatively late second-trimester abortions performed for genetic reasons is very small. It seems an almost inconsequential number, unless you happen to be one of them.

Making the medical arrangements, going back for counseling, the pretests, and finally, the abortion, was the most difficult period of my adult life. I was then twenty-one weeks pregnant, and had been proudly carrying my expanding belly. Telling everyone—friends, family, students, colleagues, neighbors— seemed an endless nightmare. But it also allowed us to rely on their love and support during this terrible time. Friends streamed in from all over to teach my classes; I have scores of letters expressing concern; the phone never stopped ringing for weeks. Our community was invaluable, reminding us that our lives were rich and filled with love despite this loss. A few weeks afterward, I spoke with another woman who'd gone through selective abortion (as this experience is antiseptically called in medical jargon). She'd returned to work immediately, her terrible abortion experience unspoken. Colleagues assumed she'd had a late miscarriage, and didn't speak about it. Her isolation only underlined my appreciation of the support I'd received.

My parents flew a thousand miles to sit guard over my hospital bed, answer telephones, shop, and cook. Filled with sorrow for the loss of their first grandchild, my mother told me of a conversation she'd had with my father. Despite their grief, they were deeply grateful for the test. After all, she reasoned, we were too young and active to be devastated like this; if the child had been born, she and my dad would have taken him to raise in their older years, so we could get on with raising other children. I can only respond with deep love and gratitude for the wellspring of compassion behind that conversation. But surely, no single woman, mother or grandmother, no single family, nuclear or extended, should have to bear all the burdens that raising a seriously disabled child entails. It points out, once again, the importance of providing decent, humane attention and services for other-than-fully-abled children and adults.

And, of course, parents of disabled children are quick to point out that the lives they've nurtured have been worth living. I honor their hard work and commitments, as well as their love, and I think that part of "informed consent" to amniocentesis and selective abortion should include information about parents' groups of Down syndrome children, and social services available to them, not just the individual, medical diagnosis of the problem. And even people who feel they could never choose a late abortion may nonetheless want amniocentesis so they'll have a few extra months to prepare themselves, other family members, friends, and special resources for the birth of a child with special, complex needs.

Recovering from the abortion took a long time. Friends, family, coworkers, students did everything they could to ease me through the experience. Even so, I yearned to talk with someone who'd "been there." Over the next few months, I used my personal and medical networks to locate and talk with a handful of other women who'd opted for selective abortions. In each case, I was the first person they'd ever met with a similar experience. The isolation of this decision and its consequences is intense. Only when women (and concerned men) speak of the experience of selective abortion as a tragic but chosen fetal death can we as a community offer the support, sort out the ethics, and give the compassionate attention that such a loss entails.

For two weeks, Mike and I breathed as one person. His distress, loss, and concern were never one whit less than my own. But we were sometimes upset and angered by the unconscious attitudes toward his loss. He was expected to "cope," while I was nurtured through my "need." We've struggled for male responsibility in birth control, sexual mutuality, childbirth, and child-rearing, and I think we need to acknowledge that those men who do engage in such transformed practices have mourning rights during a pregnancy loss, as well.

Nonetheless, our experiences *were* different, and I'm compelled to recognize the material reality of my experience. Because it happened in my body, a woman's body, I recovered much more slowly than Mike did. By whatever mysterious process, he was able to damp back the pain, and throw himself back into work after several weeks. For me, it took months. As long as I had the fourteen pounds of pregnancy weight to lose, as long as my aching breasts, filled with milk, couldn't squeeze into bras, as long as my tummy muscles protruded, I was confronted with the physical reality of being post-pregnant, without a child. Mike's support seemed inadequate; I was still in deep mourning while he seemed distant and cured. Only much later, when I began doing research on amniocentesis, did I find one study of the stresses and strains of selective abortion. In a small sample of couples, a high percentage separated or divorced following this experience. Of course, the same holds true after couples face a child's disablement, or child death. Still, I had no idea that deep mourning for a fetus could be so disorienting. Abortion after prenatal diagnosis has been kept a medical and private experience, so there is no common fund of knowledge or support to alert us as individuals, as couples, as families, as friends, to the aftermath our "freedom of choice" entails.

Which is why I've pierced my private pain to raise this issue. As feminists, we need to speak from our seemingly private experience toward a social and political agenda. I'm suggesting we lift the veil of privacy and professionalism to explore issues of health care, abortion, and the right to choose death, as well as life, for our genetically disabled fetuses. If XYLO's story, a true story, has helped to make this a compelling issue for more than one couple, then his five short months of fetal life will have been a great gift.

Bess Armstrong

Bess Armstrong was born in Ruxton, Maryland, and began acting at the age of five. She has starred in such films as *The Four Seasons*, directed and produced by Alan Alda; *High Road to China*, opposite Tom Selleck; and *Nothing in Common*, with Tom Hanks and Jackie Gleason. Most recently, she appeared in the ABC comedy series *Married People*.

Armstrong lives with her husband, John Fiedler, an independent film producer, in Los Angeles. They have two sons, ages one and four. The piece that follows was published in the Baltimore *Evening Sun* in April 1989, right after the historic pro-choice march on Washington.

In July of 1986 my daughter, Lucy, was born with an underdeveloped brain. She was a beautiful little girl—at least to me and my husband—but her disabilities were severe.

By the time she was two weeks old we knew that she would never walk, talk, feed herself, or even understand the concept of mother and father. It's impossible to describe the effect that her five-and-a-half-month life had on us; suffice it to say that she was the purest experience of love and pain that we will ever have, that she changed us forever, and that we will never cease

165

to mourn her death, even though we know that for her it was a triumphant passing.

I know that this makes me sound as if I support the anti-abortion movement. But I do not. You see, no one can tell us why Lucy was born the way she was. There was nothing genetically or chromosomally wrong with her. Her condition, we have been told over and over again, was a fluke. Consequently, no one can promise us that it won't happen again. We have been handed statistical odds that range from one in ten to one in five—and the promise that next time sophisticated ultrasound probably could pick up a problem early in the pregnancy. The choice would be a terrible one, whether or not to abort a baby so closely linked to the daughter we loved, but at least it would be ours to make.

I was asked to tell my story at a pro-choice gathering in 1989. I was to be one of several "witnesses" representing the different needs for legal abortion. It was to be an evening full of mothers and daughters united in defense of their rights, and my husband and I felt that it was the right time and place for our daughter's story to be heard.

So you can imagine how stunned I was when I found out, thirty minutes before the start of the event, that I had been cut from the list of speakers. The explanation given me was that my story, compelling as it is, was simply too dangerous to be used. It dealt with selective abortion, and some of the organizers were afraid that it would be too open to distortion by the so-called right-to-lifers.

We live in a society controlled by "sound bites," so I understand the decision that was made that night, but I don't agree with it. The decision to abort a baby isn't black and white; it is every heartbreaking shade of gray, and nothing illustrates that observation better than my story. The demand for "our rights" has ceased to be an effective rallying cry over the past fifteen years. Indeed, confronted with photos of aborted fetuses, the average American thinks the exercise of these "rights" is selfish and irresponsible.

Stories like mine are not about rights; they are about need— need, because I had to stand by helplessly while my six-pound daughter arched rigid in seizure that no medication could control; need, because she died fighting for breath in my arms. Precisely because I loved her so, shouldn't I have the right to think twice before bringing another such child into the world? The irony is that if so terrible a moment of decision comes for me, I honestly can't say what choice I will make. But I do know that no one else should have the right to make it for me.

I am not alone out here. There are thousands of mothers like me waiting to speak. To all the leaders of the pro-choice movement I say: Please, use us before it's too late. Rally the mothers of the AIDS babies, the Tay-Sachs babies, the hopelessly disabled babies like mine, and let the other side look us in the eye and tell us that ours are abortions of "convenience."

If they try to distort what we say, let's press on in any case. At this eleventh hour, our concern mustn't be about giving the other side ammunition. It must be about helping the undecided to make up their minds intelligently and with compassion.

That is what this mother and daughter wanted to say that night. I think America would have understood.

" K a t h y "

"Kathy" is the court-ordered pseudonym for the first minor who appeared in an Alabama court—in accordance with the new law—to seek a judge's permission to have an abortion without her parents' consent. At the time, which was September 1987, Kathy was nearly eighteen and working and living on her own. Both she and her mother had been abused by her alcoholic stepfather.

Judge Charles Nice of the Jefferson County Family Court denied Kathy's request for an abortion, declaring that she was not mature enough to decide for herself. In a scathing judgment, the Alabama Court of Civil Appeals overruled Nice, saying in part: "The trial court judge in this case abused his discretion by denying the minor's request. . . . We can safely say, having considered the record, that should this minor not meet the criteria for 'maturity' under the statute, it is difficult to imagine one who would." In addition, the Alabama Court of the Judiciary later found that Judge Nice had violated judicial canons of ethics in Kathy's case and suspended him without pay for six months.

When *The Choices We Made* was first published, Kathy was twenty-one, living on her own, and managing the credit department of a retail store. There was a young man in her life whom she had been seeing for more than two years. Though Kathy wanted to use her real name here, "so people would know I did something to try to help others," she felt she could not; the danger of violence from her stepfather persisted.*

I missed one period and thought, No, no, no. Then I thought, Wait a minute. I am. I let a friend go into a store and buy me a pregnancy test. I wouldn't go in because I was afraid I might see somebody I knew. I took the test, and it said that I was pregnant.

I felt like there was no way I could handle having a kid. I was

*Some details of this story have been disguised to further protect Kathy's identity. See also "Kathy's Day in Court," *Ms.*, April 1988, and "No More Mr. Nice Judge," *Ms.*, September 1988, by Angela Bonavoglia.

seventeen years old. I'd finished out my senior year, but I'd been sick a lot with real bad headaches and didn't pass a lot of things; I wanted to take my GED. I'd been working since I was fifteen, but my job as a salesgirl didn't pay that much . . . $4.75 an hour. There was no way I could support a kid.

At the time I got pregnant, my mother was staying over at my stepfather's house all the time. I lived alone in our apartment. I wish I could have talked to my mother about being pregnant, but I thought if I talked to her, my stepfather would find out, and something awful would happen. Anything that I did usually got back to him, and then he'd raise Cain about it with my mother. My stepfather was an alcoholic, so when he got drunk, he would use my mother as a punching bag. He was real violent, real bad.

Besides what my stepfather might have done if he knew I was pregnant, I couldn't tell my mother because she would have had a cow. She would have been disappointed in me . . . upset. My grandparents were real, real old-fashioned; that's the way she was brought up.

My mother got married when she was nineteen, had me the next year, and then got a divorce. She thought marrying young was a big mistake, so if she knew that I'd gotten pregnant, she'd think that was a worse mistake, and if I got an abortion, she'd probably think that was the worst mistake of all. She's not against abortion. She feels about the same way I do . . . it just depends on the situation. Sometimes I'm for it, and sometimes I'm against it. I'm against it if you can actually support a child.

I never thought about adoption. If I had carried the baby, then my stepfather would have come closer to knowing than if I'd had the abortion. Besides, I think adoption is probably more painful than having an abortion. If you do that, then your kid's somewhere wandering around in the world, and you don't know where; you'd be spending the rest of your life trying to find it.

That's not to mention what you went through when you *had* the baby—that would be just as traumatic as giving one up.

I never thought of telling my real father I was pregnant; he's not somebody I was close to. When I was little, I went over to his house every other weekend. But when I got older, my step-mother made me feel like I didn't belong in the house, and I quit going over there as much. Now, I very rarely see him.

I didn't feel like I could talk to my boyfriend. He was twenty . . . worked at a factory during the day and did his music at night. We went out for about five months. Yeah, I loved him. But I knew a girl, and she'd had an abortion. Her boyfriend didn't like the idea of it too much, and they broke up. I'm kind of insecure, and I didn't want that to happen.

I wasn't really thinking about using birth control at the time I got pregnant. I was afraid to go to a gynecologist. I tried condoms, but they usually break. The way I did it was, there's a certain time in the month when you can get pregnant—like a week in the middle—and I'd go around it. Well, my period got off so I couldn't keep up with it anymore.

I would never ask my mother about birth control, never, because she would naturally assume, "Why are you asking? Are you planning on having sex with a man?" That would have created a disappointment situation.

My friend who got me the pregnancy test in the store gave me the names of three places to call—Planned Parenthood, Sav-A-Life, and Summit Medical Center. I talked to Diane Der-zis, director of Summit Medical Center, and she told me about this new law about minors' abortions that was coming in. It was the end of the week, and the next Wednesday the law was going into effect.

She told me I could go ahead and have the abortion and how much it would cost: $210 for local anesthesia, and $260 if I got put to sleep, which I wanted—I didn't want to be awake for this.

But then Diane told me if I would wait and be the first girl to go to court and test this new law, she would do my abortion for free.

I had the money. I could have paid for the abortion, but I said okay. Everybody told me I was the perfect case because I was seventeen, lived by myself, worked, and because of everything that had happened to me. I thought, With all I've been through and I'm still here, I can handle this. I wanted to help people in the future, the people who would come up after me. By going to court, I thought I could either show people it was a terrible law or help to stop it.

Diane told me that Wendy Brooks Crew, a Legal Aid attorney, would be doing my case and wanted me to call her, so I called. I had a funny feeling because of what I was calling to talk about, but it wasn't as hard as I thought it would be because it was Wendy. She explained the law and that it was unconstitutional. We talked about the case, all the things we had to sign, what we were going to be doing in the trial, and she prepared me for the whole thing—she said she was going to get me through this.

The day of the trial I went to the courthouse myself. It's the Family Court Building in Birmingham, a big colonial-type building with columns in the front. I'd been in a courthouse before. In eighth grade, in our little civics group, we went to see all kinds of trials—murder trials, robbery trials—but we never went to see an abortion trial.

Me and Diane went upstairs and met with Wendy. We went into this big conference room, with a big humongous table with tons of chairs around it. We were sitting and talking, but then somebody came in and called Wendy out.

The next thing I know, about fifteen minutes before the trial, this man comes in and says, "I'm Marcus Jones. I'm your attorney." I was just petrified because I thought, My gosh, they're taking Wendy away from me. I said to Marcus, "Where's

Wendy? Where's Wendy?" He said, "Wendy's not going to be on your case." I said, "Why?" He said, "They took her off."*

I was so mad. I'd gotten to know Wendy. I felt like I could actually pull through this with Wendy. Then this man comes in. How is some man going to stand up there and fight for me? He knows nothing about the experience itself. He was real nice the whole time, but he didn't really know what was going on. I thought, Oh my gosh. I'm going to lose.

We asked Judge Nice if Diane could come into the courtroom, but he would not let her in. He said this was the first abortion trial, and he wanted to do things by the book—he didn't want anybody else there.

I took the witness stand. I was having heart failure. I felt so nervous, extremely nervous . . . the whole hearing just kind of passed. I remember the judge asked me whether I had thought about adoption. He kept on and on and on; he wouldn't let up on adoption. The judge asked me if the pregnancy was the result of rape or incest. I knew it wasn't the result of incest, but I couldn't remember at that moment what incest was.

I told the judge I was about ten weeks pregnant. I told him I couldn't discuss abortion with my mother because then my stepfather would find out, and he might get mad and beat up my mother.

When it was almost over, Marcus asked me if there was anything I wanted to add. I said, "Well, look. I'm here. I could have gone ahead and done this the other day. I think that shows a little bit of responsibility that I'm going through this just to make sure my abortion will be legal."

---

*Judge Nice disputed Crew's role on the case and appointed a private attorney who had never spoken to Kathy before. The finding of judicial misconduct in Kathy's case was based primarily on Nice's attempts to have the portion of the trial record that dealt with the appointment of counsel deleted before sending the record to the appeals court.

After the trial was over, Judge Nice left the courtroom. I got down off the witness stand and sat on a bench in the front row. Marcus was sitting there with me. It took the judge twenty minutes to come back out. It felt like forever.

Marcus stood up, and the judge read his little speech saying that he denied my petition. He said he didn't feel I was mature enough. He thought I should discuss it with my parents before I had the abortion. Then, he went back into his judge's chambers.

I was about in tears. I thought, How can he say this? How can he say this about me? That he didn't feel I was mature enough to make this decision myself? I was sitting there, and I could feel my eyes start pooling up. I was saying to myself, "Don't cry. Don't cry." I just don't like to cry—it makes me feel like a little kid. Sometimes I'll be sitting there with tears pouring down my face, but I will not make a sound.

After that, we discussed taking my case to the court of appeals. I thought we'd have to go through one court; I didn't think we'd have to go to the first court and then to the second. I was thinking, Oh my gosh. This thing is going to take too much time. It's going to be dangerous. If it had taken much longer, it would have been a second-trimester abortion.

I wasn't actually sorry then that I had agreed to go to court, I was just wishing that I had already gotten it over with. If the appeal didn't work, Diane said we would go to Atlanta.

I didn't talk to Diane, Wendy, or Marcus for a while. Then, I talked to Diane and asked her when they were going to court. She said they were in court that day. They called me later and told me how the court of appeals had gone, and that they had won the case.

I thought, Thank heavens. Thank heavens. We went to Marcus's office, and they asked me if I wanted to read about it. I got all the way over to the second page of the newspaper and saw what the court of appeals said about Judge Nice. I started

dying laughing! After him telling that to me? I enjoyed that
. . . I got the last laugh on him.

I told my boyfriend that I was pregnant after I went to court,
maybe the day of the appeal. He reacted about like I reacted
when I learned—confused and scared. He was in favor of the
abortion. He was going to skip work the day I went to have it,
but he'd already missed so much that I told him not to because
he might lose his job.

I went for the abortion on a Friday at one o'clock. One of my
friends took me down there and dropped me off; she left because
she had to work. I was there until about four-thirty or five
o'clock, and another girl came to pick me up.

The abortion was the most horrible experience of my life. I
saw Diane . . . she helped me through, but I felt so alone. All
through the whole thing I was wishing I could tell my mother.
Just to have her there with me, or just knowing that I could tell
her, would have made me feel better.

I had to fill out a bunch of papers, have blood taken, a urine
sample, do a little counseling thing. I was in there with two other
girls. The counselor talked to us about birth control and told us
exactly what they were going to do. I couldn't really tell you
what she said because I didn't pay attention, I didn't want to
know.

After we got out of there, she took us down a hall to a little
dressing room, and they had gowns in there. We had to change
and put all our stuff in this bag, then we had to go down this
other hall and sit in this room with about six or seven other girls
in there watching TV. They'd call us one by one and take us out.

I got in the room. I kind of knew what to expect because I'd
heard about visits to the gynecologist. There was a little table,
a little bed thing, with stirrups. Those scare me. I kept praying,
"Help me get through this, Lord. Please help me get through
this."

There were two men and a lady there. I don't know what they

were all for. I didn't care. I wanted to be put to sleep . . . to get it over with. The lady told me to get up on the table, and I did. She gave me a shot, and in about a minute, I was out. The next thing I knew, somebody was telling me to wake up.

The night of the abortion, I was supposed to rest, but I went out anyway. My boyfriend was in a band and he was playing at a fair, so I went down to see him. I didn't know when they were playing, though, and by the time I got there, it was too late.

I saw him after that night. We never really talked about the abortion . . . I didn't want to talk about it anymore either. We did break up, but not because of the abortion.

Right after the abortion, every time I saw something on TV about abortion, or if I saw a real tiny baby somewhere, I'd think, What'd I do? Sometimes I wished I hadn't done it. I didn't exactly like the idea of having an abortion. People look at you and go, "You killed a kid. You killed a life." I used to think, No, I didn't. I didn't. I didn't. . . .

I don't have those feelings at all anymore. It makes me mad when I see all the pro-life people on TV. They do not understand—there's just no way they could because they're not in everybody else's shoes. They're talking about killing things, but it's got to be a certain number of months before all the organs are formed, before it becomes a life. The pro-life people don't have their facts straight, or they're ignoring the rest of it.

I'm on the Pill now, and I've had no problems with it. In the future, I'd like to have one baby, maybe one. I want to be very in control of my life. I want to have a nice job, a husband, a decent cash flow so that I'll be able to support the kid, and a place to live.

I think parental consent laws like this one are going to get a lot of people going through the same thing I did. It scared me a lot since I had to wait so long. They made me wait fourteen days, from the hearing to the appeal, and every week you wait, it gets more and more dangerous. And these laws are going to make the state pay lawyers, so it'll cost the state a lot of its money.

Most of the time, kids will tell their parents if they're pregnant . . . it won't be in a situation like this. But I think kids know when they can tell their parents things and when they can't. Kids aren't totally stupid just because they're kids.

A F a t h e r ' s   S t o r y

The daughter of a well-known journalist was brutally gang-raped and became pregnant. Some time later, in 1981, her father told the story in one of his columns. He made that decision when he learned that members of a U.S. Senate committee, led by Jesse Helms, had voted to further restrict federal funds for poor women's abortions even when the pregnancy results from rape or incest. Below, his original column is reprinted, followed by some of his more recent thoughts about the ordeal. The story is presented here anonymously, in order to protect the identity of the daughter, as is usual with rape victims.

As for the restriction on Medicaid funding for abortions in cases of rape and incest, Congress voted for it in 1981 and President Reagan signed it into law. In 1989, Congress voted to restore the funding, but President Bush vetoed that legislation. "There were no convincing reasons given for the President to change his view," a top White House official told *The New York Times.* The restriction remained in effect until 1993.

I have been wondering whether to tell you a personal story that seems to me to have general implications. This is one of those sad family stories that normally you don't find fathers talking about in public, or even very much with close friends.

But I picked up the newspaper the other day to read that a Senate committee had voted to abolish payments for abortions for the poor, even when the pregnancies are the result of rape.

Now this was not a question of cutting the budget. Abortion costs for poor women who are raped do not amount to a large

179

sum. Rather it was a question of morality. Republican Senator
Jesse Helms of North Carolina, and the Moral Majority which
follows him around, are convinced that abortion is wrong even
when the woman who wants one wants it because she has been
raped.

So I don't think it will be very long before Jesse and his
friends are going to come after the unpoor.

In this instance, I am not very comfortable about being unpoor. I object to what the Senate committee did. But I have the
human instinct to object even more strenuously when I reason
that, by the same standard with which the senators dealt with
the poor, they will shortly deal with me.

So let me tell you my story.

A few years ago, my daughter attended an enormous Fourth
of July celebration at the Washington Monument. It was a free
show with fireworks and flags and entertainment, and, according
to the newspaper account, the large crowd behaved well.

But as my daughter strolled alone off the monument grounds
and entered a side street, a car rolled up next to the sidewalk.
Three men emerged from it, seized her roughly, and, before she
could do more than utter a half-stifled cry, put her into the
backseat, where two more men held her to the floor.

She was tied, gagged, and taken to a house, the location of
which she cannot now identify. She was kept in the house for
the rest of the night, during which time she was repeatedly
beaten and raped.

The next morning she was blindfolded, driven back to the
monument grounds, and shoved out of the car. Eventually,
sometime about midday, she made her way home.

During the time she was gone, there was, of course, a great
deal of worry and anxiety at that home. And, I must confess,
anger. Her arrival was followed by various interviews with policemen who tried to be helpful to a hysterical girl but couldn't
be, because the hysterical girl could only estimate the time she

had been in the car, describe the inside of a house, and sob out some meaningless first names.

That's really the end of the story. Except, of course, that within a very short time, my daughter knew that she was pregnant.

Now I would like to ask Senator Helms what he would do if he had been the father of the girl. I know what I did. And I can promise the senator and the Moral Majority and all the shrill voices of the right-to-life movement that no matter what law they may pass and how stringent the penalty, I would do it again.

• • •

It seems to me my first formulation of a stance on the matter of a woman's right to an abortion dates back to when I was at Dartmouth College in the late thirties. There was an episode, well known at the time and much talked about among the students because it was in the newspapers, of a girl from the Katharine Gibbs School who tried to abort herself with a coat hanger in a closet. I knew nothing about the girl except that she was going to Katharine Gibbs, a secretarial school of considerable rank and stature.

I can't remember what happened to the girl. It's embarrassing to say this, but I've forgotten if the tragedy was that she killed herself or that she was expelled from Katharine Gibbs. They seemed almost equally tragic to a sophomore's mind.

I remember feeling horror, absolute horror that this girl had to do this. I suspect even people like Dartmouth's sainted president, Ernest Martin Hopkins, must have been taken aback. But if so, the adults of the period didn't express themselves in any outrage about the law. It was just a sad and tragic event. This was, after all, a time when it was impolite to mention pregnancy, irreligious to talk of birth control, and abortion—well, that was unspeakable.

Probably my stance on abortion began there, but I can't say

that I thought it was a burning issue or that it crossed my cognizance that this was something about which citizens ought to act. Only that one incident strikes me as a searing memory.

In this instance with my daughter, I tried to put out of my mind everything that didn't have to do with the facts of the case. If you let your feelings show or take over your mind, I don't know how you'd come out. I'm not talking about the piece in the newspaper now—I'm talking about what went on in my head. Somehow setting down the facts closes the mind. Instead of emotionalizing and raging, you just put the facts down; that keeps you from crying. If you make your mind stick to the facts, you don't blow up.

My daughter was in her early twenties at the time. Right after it happened, within a couple of days, we took her to a well-known Washington hospital. People told me later there is something you can do right away that prevents impregnation. I didn't know . . . for a guy who's had children, I know less than I should.* Anyway, the doctors examined her, but they did not do anything. She came back from the hospital, and within a couple of months, we knew that she was pregnant.

As soon as we knew, there was no question in my mind about what course to take. I didn't have any feelings about murder or innocent life. That's an argument that never went through my head. I never argued with myself or with my wife. We never raised the questions that all the right-to-life ethicists raise. The fetus didn't mean anything to me. I have no love for something that was brought about by horror, terror, and attack.

These senators who have no knowledge or understanding of

---

*There is a so-called morning-after pill in use around the country, which refers to estrogen, progestin, or a combination taken within seventy-two hours of unprotected intercourse to prevent implantation or fertilization. The FDA has approved these hormones for contraception and estrogen-replacement therapy, but physicians are free to use legally marketed drugs for other indications—in this case, as a morning-after pill.

what they're talking about and who vote in committee to abolish abortions for poor people, even in cases of rape and incest, I don't think they have any morality. It's Godless, it's cruel, it's insensitive, and it's stupid. They are not seeing the human beings involved. They're not seeing love. They're not seeing affection. They're not seeing goodness of heart. They're not seeing family—they're not seeing the care of a mother and father. They're not seeing anything except some batty feeling that the only thing that matters is the unborn. They have no concern for the born—that is, my daughter, her mother, me.

My wife and I took my daughter for the abortion and brought her home. The abortion was not a traumatic experience. It was an end to a traumatic experience.

It passes through your head . . . what if she had had to carry that pregnancy to term? I don't know. Look, I'm only the father of the daughter, but how would you like to live with the constant reminder of what had happened on such and such a day, such and such number of years ago, which represented the very depths of despair and horror and fright? It doesn't seem to me that God intended that a child should remind a mother of horror, fear.

If abortion had been illegal, I would have violated the law, if I could have. I would have done *anything* to prevent her from having to carry that pregnancy to term.

The experience made me realize how important in America, in the whole world, a family is. A family is a unit, an essential unit. It's stronger in your affection, in your idea of what your values are, than your country or your city or your government or your boss or the company you work for. When it gets right down to where you stand, you stand with your family and you want to protect your family. When Senator Helms or any other people want to interfere with your family, and they represent the law, then you have to fight the law.

I suppose that's how revolutions start.

K a t h y   N a j i m y

Kathy Najimy is fast becoming a familiar face on the silver screen, appearing in a host of motion pictures, including *Sister Act* with Whoopi Goldberg, Nora Ephron's *This Is My Life, The Fisher King* with Robin Williams and Jeff Bridges, *Soapdish* with Sally Field and Kevin Kline, and *The Hard Way* with Michael J. Fox. She has also had an active stage career. Najimy won an Obie Award for her performance in the Off-Broadway hit *The Kathy and Mo Show,* which aired on HBO ·as well. She directed the Emmy Award–winning New Image Teen Theatre; soloed in *It's My Party,* her one-woman show; and participated in the San Diego Public Theatre, the feminist theater Sisters on Stage, and more than a dozen musicals. Among her current projects, Najimy is developing her own show for CBS. She lives in New York with composer John Boswell and their dog, Albert Finney.

In a monologue in *The Kathy and Mo Show*, Najimy shares her feelings about abortion, which are based on personal experience. Her story, below, begins with that monologue.

*I don't remember feeling bad.
Well no, I do. I remember not letting myself feel bad. That'd be like giving in, you know? If I let myself feel bad, it might make those people who are so against it think that they're right, like I'd be proof, a chance for them to say: "You feel* awful; *therefore, you shouldn't have done it. You're wrong." . . . So you don't think about it, because if you think about it, you might feel bad or guilty and have to give up your choice. So no, I don't remember feeling bad. It was too scary for me to feel, because then maybe they would seem right? And they're not right.*

*See, when you do something like that, you do it because for you
it is your only choice. The sad thing is you really want to be able
to feel bad about it without feeling wrong. . . .*

The biggest challenge for me in the show is doing the abortion
monologue. During the first act of the show, people are laughing
and laughing and laughing and laughing, and then the first act's
over, and they're laughing and laughing. Even though I do the
gay monologue, about an eccentric woman who finds out that her
beloved nephew is homosexual, there's still a laugh right before
the dramatic line and right after the dramatic line, just to cush-
ion it. The abortion piece is the *only* piece in the entire show,
the only forty seconds, where there is no comedy at all. It's a
challenge for the audience; it's a challenge for me.

Growing up, I was completely against abortion. I grew up in
the Catholic church. Sex outside of marriage was a sin. Birth
control was a sin. Abortion was murder. In fact, in the seventh
grade, at thirteen or fourteen, I wrote a poem that got published
in our school paper. It was called "Murder." When I heard my
friend was going to get an abortion, I was horrified, so I wrote
this poem and gave it to her. I didn't *know* anything then. I think
she still had the abortion, thank God.

I don't think I was ever really Catholic. I went to church and
did all that, and I certainly believed in God, but I never felt like
I got what they were talking about or believed it. And the things
I had in my mind were never the comforting part of religion;
they were always the things that scared me.

I wasn't sexually active until I was about eighteen. I kissed
boys at parties and stuff, but nothing really intense until I had
my first boyfriend, a very nice boyfriend. He was twenty years
old and a student. I thought I was in love.

I learned about birth control and told my mom I was going
on the Pill. I needed her to sign something. I said I needed it
to regulate my period, but she kind of knew. She signed. Sex

wasn't anything my mother and I could talk about—she's a Catholic, Lebanese woman—but she never grilled me or made me feel bad.

My mother was born in Beirut. She graduated from high school when she was fifteen. She skipped grades, went to college, and speaks four languages. But she had four kids who she stayed home and took care of, so her whole life got sidetracked. My father had two jobs, so I hardly ever saw him; he worked as a butcher during the day and as a postmaster at night for as long as I can remember, until he died when he was fifty-five. I think a lot of my feminist passion comes from seeing my mother—who was this brilliant woman, very talented, very creative—literally not have two minutes to herself.

So I'm having sex with my boyfriend. By now I'm almost nineteen, in college, and in my own apartment—this was 1976. But the relationship was fizzling. Then I think I forgot to take the Pill and had sex once that week—one time, one night—and I got pregnant.

No way could I imagine being a mother. I was in my first semester of college. I was acting, staying out all hours of the night rehearsing in different plays. I wasn't mature. I knew that I wanted to be a mother sometime—I definitely want to be a mother; I'm going to be the best mother—but not right then. By this time, I was a full-fledged feminist and knew that if I had a pregnancy I couldn't handle, I would have an abortion.

When I missed my period, I went to Health Services at San Diego State. A male friend—my best friend from the eighth grade who's still my best friend—went with me. I didn't tell my boyfriend because I didn't think he'd really understand. We weren't getting along that well, and I didn't want him to be with me just because of this. And this might sound really weird, but I didn't think it had much to do with him. If I had thought that he loved me and wanted the child, it would have been different. But I knew that he wouldn't want it—I was absolutely positive.

I had the test, and they knew immediately. This youngish doctor took me into the room and said, "Well, you're pregnant." I said, "Okay." He handed me a box of Kleenex. I said, "What's this for?" He said, "For when you cry." I said, "Well, I'm not going to cry." He said, "Well, you better take it anyway." I said, "I'm telling you—I don't need the Kleenex. Thank you very much."

Already I'm getting very defensive about the whole thing because he was expecting me to cry. I probably would have cried if he hadn't done that. Then he said, "You've gotten yourself into this, now what are you going to do?" I said, "Well, I'm going to have an abortion." He said, *"Are you sure?"* I said, "Yes." He said, "Don't you want to talk about it?" I said, "No." He said, "I think you should go into the other room to think about it." I said, "No. I don't want to think about it; I've already thought about it."

From the beginning of the experience, I was being very, very protective of women as a whole and not very protective of me. I never once let myself feel any feelings because I was so nervous that if I did, women as a whole would lose their right to abortion. I kept thinking, What if this were some other woman? What if this were a woman who was less strong, who didn't know about choice, who didn't feel good about herself, who was scared, who had parents pressuring her, who thought she was going to hell, who was younger? Another woman in this situation would have been taken advantage of. I knew that I would be one who would get away, but there would be thirty others who would sit there and cry, and he would make them feel bad—they would go kill themselves or have an illegal abortion or a baby they didn't want. He gave me the name of a doctor, and I left there without the Kleenex.

I remember sitting in my apartment one afternoon before the abortion and thinking about it. I picked up a Bible. I thought,

Well maybe there's something in here that will really inspire me and make me see that what I'm doing is right or wrong.

I cried. The tears were from a lot of guilt, Catholic guilt. When I first picked up the Bible that day, I thought, Oh, this is a sin. But I was intellectually noticing my feelings about being Catholic and thinking that abortion was wrong; I was more moved, gut level, by my own feelings of what was right and wrong. I never felt loved or cared for by that religion—I never felt like I'd been taken under its wing or protected. So I reasoned that those thoughts I was having about Catholic guilt really had nothing to do with me and who I was in my life. The part of my mind and heart that saw this decision as taking care of my life, loving me, took over.

That day, I also wondered what the abortion would be like and if I'd regret it in later years or just a week later. Would I be okay? Would it hurt? You know, it's the saddest thing. Since I started doing this piece in the show, all these pro-choice women come up to me afterwards and say they went through the same thing. They had abortions, but never let themselves feel bad and cry about it. They were afraid that if pro-choice women admitted their real feelings, they would be giving anti-choice people more ammunition to use in trying to take away our right.

The fact is that getting pregnant when you don't want to is an unfortunate, painful thing. Just the deciding—no matter what you decide—is a painful thing. Deciding to have an abortion is a painful thing. And the actual physical process of having the surgery is a painful thing. Yet, we don't allow ourselves the freedom to go to our friends and talk about it the way we would if we were going to have some other kind of surgery or break up with someone or move to another state, or if we were going through any other thing that causes pain and fear. We can't do that with our abortions, and it's such a shame.

Though I hadn't told my boyfriend yet, the night before my

abortion, I broke down. At midnight, my friend drove me to my boyfriend's house. I decided to tell him because I thought, What if I die? I knew the anesthesia would put me out during the operation—I was a little bit afraid. I went in and said to my boyfriend: "I'm pregnant. I'm going to have an abortion." He said, "Are you going to be okay?" I said, "Yes." He said, "Is there anything I can do?" I said, "No." He was really nice, but I think he was glad that I was taking care of it and not asking him to be more responsible. I don't think he had the resources—emotional or otherwise—to help.

My friend and I went to Sharp Memorial Hospital in San Diego at four in the morning. In the parking lot, there was a huge cement statue of a stork with a baby. We walked in and they had me wait thirty minutes in the same room with the women who were pregnant and waiting to have their babies. So there I was in a pink-and-blue room with baby pictures on the wall, with pelicans, storks, pregnant women, *Bride's* magazine, and *How to Name Your Baby* books. I sat there for thirty minutes, and then I said, "Let's go," and we waited outside in the parking lot.

Again I didn't think of myself. All I kept saying was, "I'm so angry at this. We have to write a letter. We have to get the name of the person who owns this hospital because if someone else would come in here, they'd run screaming." It was awful, but I never let it be awful for me, which I should have. It *was* awful for me. That I got to say, in front of 250 people, eight shows a week, those forty seconds' worth of feelings was a lot of retribution for me around my abortion.

I feel really silly telling this story because my abortion experience was Disneyland, wonderful, fantasyworld, compared to the experiences of other women. I don't want it to seem like any of this was so grueling. I had the luxury of getting a legal abortion; the only thing that was horrifying was the way people handled it, not the actual abortion.

It would be a different life right now if I'd had to have that child. I had the abortion so I could be who I was, which was Kathy. I'm sure I'd be fine with a kid somewhere, or not. Maybe I would have lost the kid. Maybe I would have had a miscarriage. Maybe I would have died in childbirth. Maybe I'd be on welfare, maybe I'd be killed somewhere in the slums of San Diego, maybe my kid would be a drug addict. I don't know. I mean, if people think the opposite of having an abortion is having a wonderful child and a lovely life, that's ridiculous.

I never really told my mom about the abortion. She's not political; she's not the most liberal, vocal woman. But her last time in New York she saw the show a lot, and I think it hit her what the abortion piece was talking about.

She never sends me a clipping unless I'm in it, but after she left she sent me a clipping from "Dear Abby." She said, "Thought you might be interested in this." The clipping is just a little letter from a Midwestern woman saying, to all the anti-choice people (based on not a terribly advanced theory, but one we hold to fastly): "I'm so tired of hearing you talk about abortions and how women shouldn't get them. I personally wouldn't get an abortion, but that's my personal choice. I would never make a law saying other women can't."

It really meant a lot to me. It was her way of saying that what I was doing was okay.

According to Jewish law, a child is considered a "person" only when it has "come into the world." The fetus in the womb is not a person until it is born. The Rabbinical principle is *lav nefesh hu*—"It is not a living soul."

Rabbi Balfour Brickner
Stephen Wise Free Synagogue,
New York, New York
Policy Council, Religious Coalition
for Abortion Rights

Every woman has a free will. God gave us free will . . . that's what separates us from the beasts. Free will is guided by conscience, and conscience is formed not only by dogma, what organized religions tell us, but by experience. A woman will answer to God for one thing: Has she followed her conscience in carrying out God's will? It's nobody's right to tell her what her conscience said to her. That's what men want to take from us . . . the right to follow our own conscience.

Sister Margaret Ellen Traxler, Director
Institute of Women Today,
Chicago, Illinois
Signed, with 24 other nuns, 1984
New York Times petition calling
for a dialogue on abortion within
the Catholic church

In my religious tradition, birth was never seen as anything but a gift, a miraculous, marvelous surprise present—a gift of God and a woman stranger. To speak of being born as a right is to jar the sensibilities and strain the moral syntax of existence. We are born of human intentions at the cost of real physical pain and the nourishing love of a woman which ought never be forced, compelled, or mandated by another person or the State.

Reverend Howard Moody, Senior Minister
Judson Memorial Church,
New York, New York
Co-founder, Clergy Consultation
Service on Abortion,
New York, New York

The Reverend
Christine Grimbol

With a fiery speech about choice at the largest pro-choice rally ever held on Long Island, the Reverend Christine Grimbol in 1989 emerged as a powerful symbol in the abortion rights movement. An ordained Presbyterian minister, Reverend Grimbol speaks out regularly and boldly about her personal experience with abortion. She is committed to giving "a language to people who already know they're pro-choice, but don't know how to reconcile their position with their faith."

Forty-seven-year-old Grimbol is pastor of the First Presbyterian Church of Sag Harbor. Her husband is pastor of the Shelter Island Presbyterian Church. They have a ten-year-old son.

My mother died in childbirth with me. When I was nine months old, my father and my three-year-old brother went fishing in upstate New York, had an accident, and drowned. At that point, where Chris would go was sort of up for grabs.

I finally went to live with my mother's older sister, who had five children. I always considered them to be my family—my mother, father, brothers and sisters. They were blue-collar, working-class. They were also American Baptists and very, very active in the church. My father was a deacon and superintendent of Sunday school, and my mother was in the Ladies Auxiliary.

While I was living with that family, I experienced an incestuous relationship with a male relative, initiated when I was six and going on until I was eleven. I didn't remember the extent to which it had happened until this year in therapy. Memories are just beginning to come back. I finally remembered that there had been actual intercourse when I was about nine years old. It was devastating to recall. I felt sad, angry . . . what came back was all the fear.

Besides the abuse from that relative, my father was very physically and emotionally abusive. I remember being hit for things like sucking my thumb; my father would be driving, turn around to slap me, and the car would swerve off the road. I never knew when he would be angry or what he would do. I was aware of the *huge* contradiction in my life in relationship to my father, who was so well respected in the church, and then would come home and beat the crap out of me.

I never thought of myself as a victim of my father or my relative because they blamed *me*. It wasn't their fault; it was my fault. That meant I couldn't let the secrets out because then everybody would know what a terrible person I was.

In terms of learning about sex, of course I learned plenty from that older relative, but I didn't know that's what I was learning. I don't remember if my mother told me or if I heard it in school, but I knew that once you got your period, you could get pregnant. When I got mine, I started avoiding him. I would never, ever be any place where I knew he would initiate anything sexual, but it took a long time for him to leave me alone.

When I was fifteen, the mother who brought me up died of brain cancer. My sister didn't trust me home alone with my father because he might hurt me, so I went to live with my mother's other sister and her family. I missed the mother who brought me up terribly and wanted to cry, but didn't. It was clear to me that if I expressed my feelings, I would be upsetting people, and that would make me the bad one, again.

From the time I was ten, I wanted to be a music teacher, and even though my grades were lousy, I really wanted to go to college. So I applied to and got accepted at Westminster Choir College in Princeton, New Jersey. After college, in 1967, I became an elementary school music teacher.

My first adult sexual experiences were in college, but when I graduated, I became extremely promiscuous. I don't know why, but I think it's common for incest victims to be promiscuous. There was a lot of unconscious stuff, but my conscious attitude was: I've done all this. What's the big deal? And I was still trying to get men to like me. I felt I had to be validated by men, which never had happened in my family. I was also drinking a lot and smoking some dope. If anybody had asked, "Chris, are you happy?" I would have said, "Absolutely. I'm so happy, nothing bothers me." I was numbing myself all over the place and didn't know it.

Never, ever did I use birth control at that time, but I was not a stupid person. I've been asking myself why. I think I know now. I was taught in church that it was bad to have sex outside of marriage, yet it was going on in my house all over the place. In my family, you did sex; you covered it up. You did sex; you didn't tell anybody about it. It was a sleazy kind of thing, and that's what it continued to be for me. As a young woman, I think it was an emotional impossibility for me to go to a doctor, a clinic, admit that I was sexually active, and ask for birth control.

I had participated in a Presbyterian church when I lived with my second aunt, so when I started teaching, I joined another Presbyterian church. The only reason I joined the church was because I liked to sing and they had a good choir; I didn't go to church unless I was paid to sing. A lot of the people there were involved in the Charismatic movement, which began in the Catholic church and then spread to all mainline denominations.

It's a neopentecostal kind of thing where people emphasize, almost overemphasize, the gifts of the spirit—laying on of hands, speaking in tongues, healing.

But the people in that church were extremely caring with me, no matter what I was saying or doing. The thing that pulled me in was that I was so needy and in so much pain. This was the first time I'd ever heard anybody pray for me by name, and touch me—literally physically touch me—in a caring way. They became my family—I don't know if I would have made it through without them. The problem was, I went from prayer group to prayer group, Bible study to Bible study; the Charismatic movement became an addiction to me.

I got pregnant when I just turned twenty-six. There was this fellow I talked to on the phone a lot, but I'd only dated him twice. On the second date I got pregnant.

I went to a regular doctor I had been to before. I set the appointment up as a checkup, and while I was there I said, "I'm afraid I might be pregnant." The doctor did the test and told me I was. This was in 1971, one year after abortion became legal in New York. My doctor was great. He spoke about abortion as an option, and said if I decided to have an abortion, he would make a referral.

I left there absolutely terrified. I felt all alone. I had no one to tell, no one to fall back on. I didn't feel I could trust anybody in either family I had lived with—physically, emotionally, financially—in any way, shape, or form. I didn't feel like the people at my church would understand; they were pretty conservative, and I felt sure that they would make me have the baby.

I talked to the man. We both agreed that getting married was out of the question, ridiculous—we'd only had two dates. And if we didn't get married, I knew I couldn't carry that pregnancy to term. I'm sure I would have lost my job, and then I wouldn't have had any money. I was a public school teacher; I bet I would lose that job today if I had a child out of wedlock. At that time, even if I wouldn't have lost my job, I couldn't have taught and gotten help to take care of a baby, not on a teacher's salary. The man said he would prefer for me to have an abortion.

I didn't want to have an abortion, but I didn't want to have a baby either. It seemed to me abortion was the only choice I could possibly make and carry on my life. But I was scared because I thought I might be punished for it by never getting pregnant again. I was ready to throw myself out a window. I was as close to suicide as at any time in my life.

I called the doctor back, and he gave me the name of a doctor at Flower Fifth Avenue Hospital. I set up the appointment for a week from then. During that week, the man came down to my house every night and stayed with me until I went to sleep. I was so scared, and he had enough caring not to want me to be alone.

He also paid for the abortion, $650. It could have been cheaper if I had wanted to go to a clinic, but I didn't. I had all these things looming over me . . . the procedure was so new, my mother had died in childbirth, and I'd seen an illegal abortion, which was horrible. My friend went to somebody who stuck rods up her, and then she had to just wait for the fetus to be expelled from her body. I was with her. It was so painful for her . . . she just screamed and screamed. She finally passed it, and it looked like a great big kidney bean. The whole thing was terrifying. I wanted to be in a place where I would get the absolute best care possible . . . I wanted to be in a hospital.

So I went to Flower Fifth Avenue. The doctor was real good to me. I think I had a vacuum aspiration, and I was knocked out. As a matter of fact, I remember coming to in the recovery room, and this bothers me to this day. I was kind of in la-la land, and the nurses were trying to get me to relax by asking me questions like, Where do you live? What do you do for a living? And here I was telling them. It was so early on in terms of abortion's being legal that I wonder if the nurses just hadn't been trained very well yet, but I remember thinking, Why are they getting me to tell them this? How am I to know that this nurse isn't going to be the cousin of somebody on my staff? But I could not stop myself from babbling . . . I was not in control.

I remember the doctor saying to me that day, before the abortion, "The hardest part is over." I said, "What do you mean?" He said, "The decision to be here." I don't think he was right. The hardest part for me was after the abortion. I felt real ashamed. Even though abortion was legal, I felt the only people who approved were me, my doctor, and this man who was involved with me. I felt the few other people who knew were thinking, "It's over. Let's pretend it never happened. Let's never talk about it." I had no way to deal with what I had just done. The abortion became another secret in my life.

After the abortion, the doctor said, "You have to use contraception. If you want to come back here for a class, you can, for free." I never went back, I guess because I didn't know what I would find there, maybe other "bad" people. The fellow and I continued to date after the abortion, but we started using condoms. I did insist on men using condoms after that. I don't remember risking pregnancy again.

As the years went by, I stopped drinking in bars; I wasn't doing drugs; the promiscuity eased off. I put everything into this one funnel . . . the Charismatic church. I became one of these very obnoxious praise-the-Lord-ers. Oh, God, I was constantly going to Bible studies, constantly talking about Jesus. It put me on another level where I didn't have to deal with being human. Not being human was my goal. It was too painful to be human.

I decided to go to Princeton Theological Seminary because I was involved in this whole Charismatic thing and because I had been restless in teaching for a while. I planned to work in the arts in the church, and went to seminary in 1973 to get a two-year master of arts degree. But when I got there, I saw what women were doing. I saw that if I only went for one more year and got ordained, I could do whatever I wanted. By then I was realizing that the pews were filled with people like me who had experienced a lot of pain; I thought I would be a good minister. I changed from the master of arts to the master of divinity degree.

The summer after my first year at seminary, I went to work as a student chaplain. I also began therapy. Then, I had a total faith crisis. I realized that I was probably one of the most enraged human beings that I had ever known in my life, I had not prayed away anything, and nothing was permanent, including my faith. The result of that crisis was that I discarded some of the things from my Charismatic experience that were no longer relevant, including trying to get buoyed up all the time, staying on what I called an "Easter high." I started realizing that as a Christian, I had to pull in Good Friday; I had to be human, feel the pain, and believe that I would not go crazy.

At that point in my life, I also became involved in the seminary's women's center because they had a couple of programs that were interesting, including a program on abortion. I wanted to be there because I thought to myself, Do I believe in choice? Do I believe that it's okay to have an abortion because I had one, or that it's okay theologically, faith-wise?

It was so new at that point to talk about abortion on a seminary campus. I never said that I'd had an abortion, but I was real adamant about the subject. Everyone was bringing up these horror stories about abortion, saying things like, "What if you're a twelve-year-old?" "What if you're fourteen?" "What if you're raped?" And I'm thinking, Yeah, but what if you're just twenty-five, and you're a teacher, and you'll lose your job, and you have nothing else you can do and no one to fall back on? I kept bringing up what I thought were more usual situations, and I said, "That's enough of a reason."

The Presbyterian church's official stand on abortion is pro-choice. It's been challenged every year for a long time, but every year we stand firm. Part of the stand is based on stewardship, on the belief that our job as human beings is to take care of the world and if we have babies we can't take care of, that is not particularly moral.

I would add even more than our official statement. I believe—and this is a common Christian paradox—that the kingdom of God has come, is here, and is yet to come. The kingdom of God is present when we can see the action of God in the world, when we can see compassion and mercy and love at work. But the kingdom of God is not yet here in all the also obvious ways . . . poverty, war, incest, child abuse, rape, homelessness, and hunger in the most wealthy country in the world.

I believe that as Christians, we are called to usher in the kingdom of God. We do that by insisting that these issues be addressed. Choice has to be connected to that. Life for a Christian is more than breathing in and out. Until people have a home in which to raise their children, the safety and security of whatever they need to do that well, then abortion needs to be a choice. Clearly, giving a woman the right to abortion is a compassionate stand, and anytime compassion rules over judgment, we see the kingdom of God.

I can't get any of these Bible-thumping, anti-abortion people to show me any place in all Scripture where Jesus ever says, "You made your bed, now lie in it. Too bad. Tough." I don't think Jesus is going to say, "Yep, mother took cocaine. Tough. Let this baby be born. Let it suffer for three weeks unbearably, and then die."

I see Jesus being outrageously gracious, outrageously forgiving. If Jesus were right here today, I think he would say, "I'm sad that anyone has to have an abortion. I'm sad that that has to be a choice. But you've been created as human beings . . . you're going to make mistakes. Yes, I do value life, I do value babies, but I don't use babies for punishment. And you've had a lot of babies born that you haven't taken care of very well. I want you to find homes for these children that have been battered and abused. I want you to get these people off the streets. I want you to take care of what you've already got."

I'm probably only beginning to know what risks I'm taking by speaking out on abortion. There are people who would rather I not do this. Some write to me and say, "I'm praying for your soul."

After the *Webster* decision, I thought I'd really kept too silent on the subject. I decided that I would commit myself to speaking out whenever I was asked. I find it helps with people that I can say, "I'm not just talking theory here." And it helps me . . . I don't want the secrets anymore.

About the Author

Angela Bonavoglia is an award-winning journalist and author, nationally recognized for her work in the field of reproductive health. She received an Exceptional Merit Media Award (sponsored by Radcliffe College and the National Women's Political Caucus) for health reporting for her article on the issues surrounding late abortion. Her investigation into one of the country's first prosecutions of a pregnant woman for fetal abuse was nominated for a National Magazine Award. In addition to serving as a *Ms.* contributing editor, Ms. Bonavoglia has written about social, health, and women's issues for *Mirabella*, *Redbook*, *Cosmopolitan*, the *Chicago Tribune*, *Child*, and *Newsday*, among other publications. She also has served as a policy analyst and communications consultant to the nation's major reproductive health organizations.